Published by Out-Spoken Press,
Future Studio,
237 Hackney Road,
London, E2 8NA

All rights reserved
© Giovanni Quessep

Translation Copyright
© Felipe Botero Quintana & Ranald Barnicot

The right of Giovanni Quessep to be identified
as the author of this work has been asserted by
him in accordance to section 77of the Copyright,
Design and Patent Act 1988.

A CIP record for this title is available from
the British Library.

This book is in copyright. Subject to statutory
exception and to provisions of relevant collective
licensing agreements, no reproduction of any
part may take place without the written permission
of Out-Spoken Press.

First edition published 2018
ISBN: 978-1-9996792-1-7

Design & Art Direction
Ben Lee

Printed & Bound by:
Print Resource

Typeset in: Baskerville

Out-Spoken Press is supported using public
funding by the National Lottery through
Arts Council England.

A Greek Verse for Ophelia
& Other Poems

Giovanni Quessep

Selected Poems

1968–2017

Translated by
Felipe Botero Quintana & Ranald Barnicot

A voice in contemporary migration
by Felipe Botero Quintana

The book you hold in your hands is a rare thing: the poetry it contains is the result of the improbable encounter between faraway cultures, literatures, fantasies, fables and characters before the era of virtual globalization brought on by the Internet. It is a mixture of different poetic traditions and different dream-like worlds. The very title of the book suggests it: a Greek verse (which indeed it is, with its subtle references to Penelope and the constant evocation of those "Mediterranean clear waters") for Ophelia, a legendary Danish noblewoman famous for her role in a tragedy written by a certain English playwright.

However, this mixture of historically distant European literary sources is just one part of the story. On the other hand, we find a Lebanese family forced to emigrate from their homeland at the end of the nineteenth century because of economic hardship, religious intolerance and colonialist military interference from the Ottoman, French and British empires. On their way to a better place (which could have been Brazil, the United States or simply anywhere in that hemisphere which received repeated waves of immigration at the beginning of the twentieth century), they disembark in a Colombian port (Cartagena) and are robbed of the scarce money they have brought with them. This "little service", as the poet would put it many years later, forces them to settle down somewhere near the coast where distant members of their family are already trying their luck and discovering a prosperous market for commerce. Two generations later, a boy grows up in a tiny Colombian town, almost new and invisible on the map, which can only be reached by canoe and where his father is opening the first cinema hall whilst at the same time trying to teach his son the language of his ancestors. Though he fails at this enterprise, both he and his mother (Quessep's grandmother, Venut Chadid) did manage to impress upon his son a strong image of the world they came from, which he will later complete through literary sources: the gardens of the Koran and Omar Khayyam, the fantastic creatures that dwell in Persian epic poetry, Scheherazade's endless tales and the discourses on love by Arab Andalusian poets such as Ibn Hazm.

To our great fortune, there are many artistic and cultural expressions which have preserved the magical and provincial atmosphere of those small, difficult to reach villages near the Atlantic Coast in the first half of the twentieth century, when Giovanni Quessep was born. For instance, the old *vallenatos*, the typical music form of the Colombian Caribbean, which convey so well the folkloric legends of the time as well as the general attitudes of joy, romance and carefree living but also fearful, almost medieval religiosity and political narrow-mindedness. Obviously no one captured this extraordinary ambience better than Gabriel García Márquez and his *magnum opus, One Hundred Years of Solitude*. It is no wonder Quessep worships him, devoting one of his most famous poems to his novel ('The lark and the scorpions', included in this selection). The greatest achievement of the Colombian Nobel Prize-winner was to capture with poetic precision the general spirit of magic realism that enveloped the political, social and economic evolution of these small communities, almost detached from the rest of the world, on the Colombian North Coast. Quessep's poetry is as infused with this unique historical atmosphere as García Márquez's narrative is, since both of their works are transversally determined by their experience of growing up in one of those small towns whose literary archetype has become forever the magical and tragic Macondo of García Márquez's novel.

Nonetheless, there is one key difference in the manner in which these writers approach the "Macondean" subject: whereas García Márquez's novel is written from the standpoint of the village founders, the native dwellers who view "foreigners" with a strange mixture of openness and distrust and with whom they will only progressively get involved later on, as they become part of their community, much of Quessep's poetry appears to be born from the experience of the traveller, the forced or voluntary rambler who stumbles upon his way on marvels which he had been unaware of and which he greets with fascination. As Nicanor Vélez writes in his introduction to the *Metamorfosis del Jardín*:

> ... the foreigner is someone coming from outside and who sees it all *for the first time*; that is to say, he sees what the *local inhabitants* do not see because everyday life has the tendency to cloud what recurs (...) in the passing days. It is thus that wonder manifests its capacity to make visible the *invisible*.[1]

Quessep was a "foreigner" in San Onofre, his own native town, on two counts: on the one hand, because of his father's Middle Eastern provenance but also on account of his mother, Paulina Esguerra, who came from Bogotá, Colombia's capital. Back then, as García Márquez' character Fernanda del Carpio demonstrates so comically, a person coming from Bogotá to the Caribbean Coast could be perceived as no less foreign and out of place than a person coming from Lebanon, perhaps even more so. The difference in climate, the distance made almost unsurmountable by the precariousness and scarcity of the roads, the rigidity of social structures derived from Spanish colonialism and the contrast between the burgeoning, modern, cement city made in the image of the European capitals and the newly founded village closer to nature, where everyone was at the outset equally poor, must have made these two communities, though belonging to the same nation, seem universes apart. And yet we must not think of Quessep's mother as the frivolous, snobbish character on whom García Márquez vents his low opinion of the people of Bogotá: if for nothing else because, according to him, she gifted her son with a love of poetry and familiarity with the work of Spanish and Latin American Romantics and Modernists such as Rubén Darío and Antonio Machado, adding thus more elements to the melting

---

1   Nicanor Vélez, 'Del exilio al arraigo: la poesía de Giovanni Quessep', in: Quessep, G. (2007). *Metamorfosis del jardín: Poesía reunida, 1968-2006* (N. Vélez, Ed.). Barcelona: Galaxia Gutenberg Círculo de Lectores, p. 32.

pot in which his poetry would later brew.

Not long after the Quessep family had settled in San Onofre they were forced back on the road, this time because of Colombia's internal political violence. Just as García Márquez's Macondo gets rapidly and voraciously sucked into the unrelenting fratricidal conflict between liberals and conservatives that had characterized Colombia's political evolution since its independence from Spain, the Quessep family was soon dragged into it as well: in 1949, when the poet was ten years old, his family was the first to be expelled from San Onofre by conservative authorities, due to Luis Enrique's (the poet's father) liberal convictions. They were one of many displaced families to follow for, according to present-day historians, the Colombian historical period known as *La Violencia* left around three hundred thousand dead and more than two million forced migrants, a refugee crisis which affected a fifth of the national population at the time, in a period of a little over a decade. Indeed, this could be the "time dispossessed by fables" that Quessep refers to in 'In between trees', a poem that many of his commentators have interpreted to be his most "political", possibly riddled with symbolic references to Colombia's internal conflict. Another "foreigner" raised in the Colombian Caribbean Coast, Alejandro Obregón, the half-Catalan half-*barranquillero*[2] painter, left a heart-wrenching testimony of this horrifying outburst of political violence: his masterpiece, titled simply *Violence*, "is for Colombians what *Guernica* or *The Scream* are for the world: images that synthesize the horror, the despair, the barbaric behavior that human beings are capable of", as a Colombian writer would later describe it.[3]

Therein lies the reason that the "foreigner" often present in Quessep's poems is also an "exile", a condition that adds to the fascination of the encounter with the new a bitter nostalgia for the world one has been obliged to leave behind. This is a bitterness made deeper by the encounter with the other crude and familiar aspect of migration: discrimination. When the Quessep family reached the Colombian coast, they discovered with dismay that

---

2   The name received by the people of Barranquilla, a city port that was and continues to be one of the main economic, cultural and political capitals of the Colombian Atlantic Coast.

3   Samper Pizano, D. (January 23th 2014). *Violencia*, Alejandro Obregón. *Revista Arcadia* (100), p.27.

they would from then on receive the generalizing epithet of "the Turks", a name which was particularly hateful for the Lebanese because it was precisely an invasion by the Ottoman Empire and its religious persecutions which had forced them out of their land. And in both Sincelejo and Cartagena, cities where Quessep would finish his primary and secondary education after leaving San Onofre, he would find that "there were certain places, where my friends went, that I couldn't go because they said, 'Turks are not accepted here'"[4] and that it was frowned upon for a "Colombian" woman to date someone of Arab descent.

Such encounter with discrimination would beget another great protagonist of Quessep's poetry: solitude, the loneliness of the traveller in a foreign land once he has discovered its darkest, most disappointing aspects, which for that reason will later coincide, at least partially, with the loneliness of the disenchanted lover, as Ulysses seems to be in the 'Imaginary letter' he writes to Nausicaa (also included in this selection). And indeed, isn't the confrontation with discrimination sufficient to make a person long for his home, no matter how beautiful and enchanting the new landscapes he has stumbled upon? Isn't it sufficient to fall out of love? In Quessep's poetry disenchantment occupies a central space. It is almost always followed by a yearning gaze directed towards the past, often an idealized past that never truly existed, just as the home of the exiled traveller has ceased to exist after his departure. The Garden of Eden never was, Quessep appears to hint in some of his poems. But neither is Ithaca anymore, for it has already changed beyond recognition, or "She has nothing left to give you now", as Cavafy, another of Quessep's important poetic references, puts it. I believe that this combination of exile, discrimination, disenchantment and yearning for idealized or mythological origins is the true meaning of the definition of nostalgia that Quessep provides in the first poem you'll find in this collection: "to live without remembering/ the word we are made of".

---

4   Nicanor Vélez, 'Del exilio al arraigo: la poesía de Giovanni Quessep', in: Quessep, G. (2007). *Metamorfosis del jardín: Poesía reunida, 1968-2006* (N. Vélez, Ed.). Barcelona: Galaxia Gutenberg Círculo de Lectores, p. 13.

It is perhaps from such disenchantment that springs the need for fables, myths, legends but also music, which in Quessep's work is almost always synonymous with art and poetry in general. The title of what he now considers his first book is very telling in this respect: *Being is not a fable*. In Quessep's poetry there seems to be a perpetual dichotomy, not between "good and evil", but rather between reality (being) and poetry (fable), the desert and the garden.[5] Art in general seems to arise as remedy against the hard facts of existence: death, sorrow, pain, exile, the end of love, but also oblivion as the final fate of everything that is. Many of Quessep's poems are infused with an almost painful awareness of time, of how fleeting things are and how eventually we will all share the same void, which is "The days and things without us" (in 'What we ignore', another of the poems included in this selection). Again, we must return to the image of the traveller, taking it this time in its most abstract significance: that of existence as a brief voyage between birth and death.

But in the face of this brevity and the voyage's hardship, which can provoke disenchantment in the traveller, human communities have historically responded with creation, with invention. Not only to improve the conditions of our existence but also to tell each other of our particular voyage in life, embellishing stories with metaphors and symbols and sometimes building them up into myths or moralizing tales: fables from which we hope that those who will follow us in this path will extract some knowledge or at least a sense of beauty, of awe. This in turn can also start a dialogue between the living and the dead, as Quessep's poem 'To Venture into the past' beautifully insinuates. In any case, by creating, by inventing, we do not seek to deny or condemn life, nor do we look to triumph over or "conquer" death, for ultimately our creations, our fables, myths and music are bound for oblivion as well, as Quessep's poetry frequently suggests. What we seek is rather to complement being, to enrich reality, what already

---

5 "Al-Mutamid, King of Seville, said that the true poet is always looking, simultaneously, to a garden and a desert": a statement made by Quessep in *Oficio de poeta* (edited by Rosita Jaramillo), which is considered to be a declaration of aesthetic principles and the origin of the title of his seventh book, *A garden and a desert* (1993). Nicánor Velez says that, though he and many of Quessep's readers "fell for [this] trap" (p.43), he would later discover the famous quote by the King of Seville to be Quessep's own invention.

is, with what we ourselves create and bring upon this world, in the same manner that cultures and nations are complemented, indeed enriched, by the "foreigners" they receive and the creations and life conceptions they bring with them.

This book of poetry is a celebration of cultural diversity, confrontations with the new and the different which the traveller finds on the way and then contrasts and merges with elements of where he or she comes from, of what he or she is. Being the first volume of Quessep's work ever to be published in English, it cannot but aspire to produce the same sort of enriching encounters between unsuspected figures, backgrounds and cultural traditions as those out of which Quessep's own poetry is born. It is a voice in the polyphonic choir our world has become thanks to contemporary migration. A voice in contemporary migration hoping to awake another voice, another fable, another voyage…

Note on the translation
by Ranald Barnicot

First of all, here is a quotation which has become a cliché, no doubt, but is still very much part of current debate:

"Poetry is what gets lost in translation." — Robert Frost

To this, the following rejoinder has frequently been made: poetry is what is *gained* in translation.

In translation, is poetry lost or gained? This, I would argue, depends very much on two factors: the difficulty of the original poem and the quality of the translator (or, in the case of this selection, translators).

Some poetry is, *perhaps*, untranslatable. I once read an online article in French (which, unfortunately, I can no longer trace) about an attempt to translate into that language Dylan Thomas's 'And Death Shall Have No Dominion'. The result, as the translator freely admitted, was a not very good French poem. But notice that I have italicised the word "perhaps". Was the translation a failure simply because the original poem was too difficult, or might another translator have done better? Translations which are complete or relative failures pose interesting challenges for subsequent translators.

Then there's another, related, issue. Should a translation be close to the original, even literal, or may it be free? There is a risk that the former may be an accurate representation of the original but lacking poetic quality – a mere 'crib', in fact. The latter carries the opposite risk: that the translator has merely exploited the original to write his or her own poem 'on its back'.

I would point out that a literal translation, if it complies with the grammatical and stylistic requirements of the target language, need not lack poetic quality. What is the most famous half-line of English translation? Perhaps the opening of John Dryden's translation of Virgil's *Aeneid*: "Arms and the man I sing ...". But this is in fact a literal translation of the Latin *"Arma virumque cano ..."* So perhaps Dryden's half-line is not in itself original, yet his translation is, in my view, perfect in this case.

Many of our translations are quite literal. Let's take the last four lines of 'In memory's unbeing' in *Being is not a fable*, Quessep's first book:

Today silence leads us to another
fate, memory's unbeing.
The sky passes to shadow, the wind passes.
Here is a sun purer than death.

Readers with knowledge of Spanish will appreciate that this is a fairly close translation of the original:

Hoy el silencio nos conduce al otro
destino, en el no ser de la memoria.
El cielo pasa en sombra, pasa el viento.
Aquí hay un sol más puro que la muerte.

At other times we have been much freer. This is particularly so in translating rhymed poetry into rhymed poetry, which we have done as consistently as possible. For example, these three lines from 'Si se nombra la blancura' ('If whiteness is named'), the second 'décima' in the second book, *Duration and Legend*:

Hilo de la muerte florida
Que va tejiéndole el fin
Mano que ha sido jardín

are rendered by us as:

Thread of a flowery death begetting
That still its end continues weaving
Hand that's been a garden waving

The last line of the Spanish just means "Hand that's been garden". Our motivation in adding 'waving' was firstly to provide a half-rhyme for 'weaving', thus preserving the rhyme-scheme of the original. However, there's an additional, poetic, justification in that it amplifies the image of the garden, flowers and trees waving in the breeze, and also waving a greeting and a farewell, which is very much the theme of the poem: that language, memory and life itself collaborate in their own dissolution.

We have also departed from the original even when rhyme is not involved, to produce aesthetic effects which do not distort the sense of the original. For example, in *'Un verso griego para Ofelia'* ('A Greek verse for Ophelia') we have:

"Apenas quise
dejar que entrara el trovador que hacía
agua y laúd y flor de la madera."

(Literally: "I hardly wished to allow the troubadour to enter who made water and lute and flower from wood.")

We have translated it as follows:

"Indeed I grudged
the troubadour, transmuting wood
to water, flower and lute, entry."

Our version contains effects of assonance and alliteration, but in content is not far removed from the original.

On the subject of rhyme, much of the rhyme in the original is assonantal (this has been a feature of Spanish-language poetry ever since the early medieval epic *El Cantar Del Mío Cid*). We have reflected this to the best of our ability.

This has been a fruitful and stimulating collaboration between two poet-translators, each working on far distant continents. There have clearly been disagreements about how to translate certain lines, but in every case an acceptable compromise has been reached. I am very grateful to Felipe Botero Quintana for introducing me to this difficult, mysterious, elusive and allusive poet, who nevertheless has the power of transmuting his melancholy and elation into words that can, as Eliot put it, communicate before they are understood. Indeed, the meaning of these poems often cannot easily be summed up. However, the more one reads, the more one finds oneself, somehow, within them.

A Greek Verse for Ophelia & Other Poems

Contents

28	**From *Being is not a fable*** *El ser no es una fábula*, 1968
29	Mientras cae el otoño / As autumn falls
31	Materia sin sonido de amor / Matter without the sound of love
33	En el no ser de memoria / In memory's unbeing
35	Lo que ignoramos / What we ignore
37	Cuando dijo su nombre / When he said his name
39	El ser no es una fábula / Being is not a fable
41	Con dura transparencia / With hard transparency
43	Canción para el final / A song for the end
45	El mar y los amantes / The sea and the lovers
48	**From *Duration and legend*** *Duración y leyenda*, 1972
49	Epitafio del poeta adolescente / Epitaph of the adolescent poet
51	Para grabar a la entrada del jardín destruido / To engrave at the gates of the destroyed garden
53	Paraíso perdido para el poeta / A poet's paradise lost
55	En la luna he contado / In the moon I have told
57	Alguien se salva por escuchar el ruiseñor / Someone is saved by listening to the nightingale
59	La alondra y los alacranes / The lark and the scorpions
61	Si se nombra la blancura / If whiteness is named
64	**From *Song of a foreigner*** *Canto del extranjero*, 1976
65	Madrigal / Madrigal
67	A la sombra de Violeta / To Violeta's shade
73	Elegía / Elegy
77	Lectura de Omar Khayyam / Reading of Omar Khayyam
79	Canto del extranjero / Song of a foreigner

86	**From *Madrigals of life and death*** (*Madrigales de vida y muerte*, **1978**)
87	Quiero apenas una canción / I want merely a song
89	Me pierde la canción que me desvela / I am lost by the song that keeps me awake
91	Callar es bello / To be quiet is beautiful
93	En el jardín profundo / In the deep garden
95	En soledad escrito / In solitude written
97	Azules de otra luna / Blues from another moon
99	Escrito para ti, en tu nombre / Written for you, in your name
101	El que no ha de contar su fábula / Who shall not tell his fable
104	**From *Preludes*** (*Preludios*, **1980**)
105	Elegía / Elegy
107	Quizá todo ha pasado / Perhaps everything has passed
109	Quien ama la melodiosa penumbra / Who loves the melodious gloom
111	La culpa / Guilt
113	Aventurarse en el pasado / To venture into the past
115	Para hacerte a la música / To become one with music
117	Primera maravilla / First wonder
120	**From *Death of Merlin*** (*Muerte de Merlín*, **1985**)
121	Insomnio / Insomnia
123	Canción del que parte / Song of the departing
125	Por la vida desesperada / Through the desperate life
127	Del color de otra orilla / Of the colour of another shore
129	Puerto / Port
131	La ronda de la vida / The round of life
133	Gris deseante / Wishing grey
135	Joya abolida para el alma / An abolished jewel for the soul
137	Canción del exiliado / Song of the exiled
139	Nada perdura en la memoria / Nothing lasts in memory
141	Lectura de William Blake / Reading of William Blake
143	Metamorfosis del jardín / Metamorphoses of the garden
145	Entre árboles / In between trees
147	Muerte de Merlín / Death of Merlin

150	**From *A garden and a desert*** (*Un jardín y un desierto*, **1993**)
151	Pájaro / Bird
155	Desvanecerse / To fade
157	Última canción de Orfeo / Orpheus' last song
159	Piedra blanca / White rock
161	Salmo y epigram / Psalm and epigram
163	Tejido / Thread
165	Un verso griego para Ofelia / A Greek verse for Ophelia
169	Por ínsulas extrañas / Amidst strange islands
172	**From *Imaginary letter*** (*Carta imaginaria*, **1998**)
173	Cuerda de oro / String of gold
175	Del arte y el destino / Of art and fate
177	Grabado en la piedra / Engraved in the stone
179	Navegantes / Sailors
181	Oración de los cazadores / The hunters' prayer
183	Ars amandi / Ars amandi
185	Carta imaginaria (*de Ulises a Nausícaa*) / Imaginary letter (*from Ulysses to Nausicaa*)
192	**From *The starless air*** *El aire sin estrellas*, **2000**
193	Adonaí / Adonai
195	Cuerpo cantado / Sung body
197	Canción de bodas / Wedding song
199	Sibila / Sybil
201	Un vino triste / A sad wine
203	Visión / Vision
206	**From *Lunar ember*** *Brasa lunar*, **2004**
207	El puerto del almendro / The almond port
209	Diamante / Diamond
211	Brasa del silencio / Ember of silence
213	Después será el vacío / Hereafter the void
215	Sonata / Sonata
217	Juicio final / Final judgement
219	Monólogo de Sherazada / Scheherazade's monologue

222	**From *Leaves of the Sybil*** *Las hojas de la Sibila*, 2006
223	Polvo y grana / Dust and grass
225	Cántico de la piedra / Canticle of the rock
227	La hora de vivir / The hour of living
229	No florece la piedra / The rock does not bloom
231	Oropéndola / Oriole
233	Simurg / Simurgh
235	No des paz a tu reino / Do not give peace to your kingdom
237	Nocturno / Nocturnal
239	Cuento del paraíso / Paradise story
242	**From *The artist of silence*** *El artista del silencio*, 2012
243	Telar con pájaros y hojas / Loom of birds and leaves
245	Invitación / Invitation
247	Palabras que ya fueron / Words that already were
249	Apariciones / Apparitions
251	Versos del silencio / Verses of silence
253	La última orilla / The last shore
255	El artista del silencio / The artist of silence
258	**From *Abyss unveiled*** *Abismo revelado*, 2017
259	Oración / Prayer
261	Sortilegio / Spell
263	De cedro y de ciprés / Of cedar and cypress
265	Abismo revelado / Abyss unveiled
267	Naufragio / Shipwreck

A Greek Verse for Ophelia & Other Poems

Being is not a fable
El ser no es una fábula

1968

La mer, la mer, toujours recommencée.
Paul Valéry

Mientras cae el otoño

Nosotros esperamos
envueltos por los hojas doradas.
El mundo no acaba en el atardecer,
y solamente los sueños
tienen su límite en las cosas.
El tiempo nos conduce
por su laberinto de horas en blanco
mientras cae el otoño
al patio de nuestra casa.
Envueltos por la niebla incesante
seguimos esperando:
La nostalgia es vivir sin recordar
de qué palabra fuimos inventados.

As autumn falls

Shrouded in golden leaves,
we wait.
The world doesn't end at sunset
and only dreams
limit themselves to things.
Through a labyrinth of blank hours
time leads us on
as autumn falls
over our house, our patio.
Shrouded in a relentless fog
we wait, we wait:
nostalgia means to live without remembering
the word we are made of.

Materia sin sonido de amor

Vamos perdiendo cielo. Nos acosa
la alta noche. Soñamos y perdemos.
Los dados falsos, las huecas imágenes
en la tierra. ¿Algún día no fue nuestro
el mar, su ciclo de labios y pájaros,
su complicado amor, el son eterno
de su discordia? Turbias soledades.
Miramos esta luz y vuelan hojas
o nunca ya sin nombre de no ser
la transparencia, tocamos el tiempo
ya tan nosotros, ya tan nada, tan
palabra caída en loca hermosura.
Vamos perdiéndonos, precipitándonos
de esperanza. Materia sin sonido
de amor, materia aislada de los sueños
y el bosque de hadas en la húmeda noche.
Todo el resto es camino. ¿Dios? Silencio.

Matter without the sound of love

We are losing sky as we go. The high night
stalks us. We dream and we lose.
The false dice, the hollow images
of the earth. Were they not ours for a day,
the sea, with its cycle of lips and birds,
its complicated love, discord's
eternal hum? Murky solitudes.
We look at this light and leaves fly by,
or – now transparency
unnamed no longer nor robbed of its being –
we touch time
now so much us, now so much nothing, so much
fallen among crazed beauty of words.
We're losing ourselves as we go, hurling along
in hope. Matter without the sound
of love, matter isolated from dreams
and in the humid night the fairy woods.
All the rest's road and roads. God? Silence.

En el no ser de la memoria

Hoy el silencio se hace nuevamente
discordia; como un reino del otoño
que se abre ante nosotros, de su orilla
nublada al laberinto de las cosas.
La espuma irrefutable, el mar en tierra.
Nunca fuera su don clara derrota
si fuese menos tiempo, pero ahueca
pájaros, lluvia, arremolina sueños
y claridad, carcome las palabras
hasta el temor y la mala esperanza.
Hoy el silencio nos conduce al otro
destino, en el no ser de la memoria.
El cielo pasa en sombra, pasa el viento.
Aquí hay un sol más puro que la muerte.

In memory's unbeing

Today is silence made discord
anew; like an autumn kingdom
opening up to us, it gives its
cloudy rim to the labyrinth of things.
The irrefutable foam, the sea on land.
Never would its gift be such a clear defeat
had it lasted less but it hollows out
birds and rain, swirls dreams around
with clarity, withers words
until they become fear and malignant hope.
Today silence leads us to another
fate, memory's unbeing.
The sky passes to shadow, the wind passes.
Here is a sun purer than death.

Lo que ignoramos

Aquí no hay un celeste. Nunca. Llegas
empujado por días, por palabras,
por el viento que sube del otoño
dándote niebla, lluvia entre los pasos.
Sólo tu negación. El tiempo. Siempre
se te podrá cantar: la vida no es
el volumen de ser en lo que sueñas.
La vida es esto que madura en sombra.
¿Quién se vuelve destino, piedra, fecha?
¿Quién va de nunca a olvidado mañana?
Lo que ignoramos, ay, lo que sabemos
entre voces perdidas en el polvo.
Cruda esperanza que incendia la piel.
Los días y las cosas sin nosotros.

What we ignore

Here there is no sky blue. Never. You come
impelled by days, by words,
wind rising out of autumn
providing you its fog, rain between footsteps.
There is only your denial. Time. You can always
be sung to: life is not
the volume of being in your dreams.
Life is this ripening in the shadow.
Who can become destiny, stone, date?
Who goes from never to oblivion's morrow?
What we ignore, oh, we know amid
dustlost voices.
Raw hope, incinerating skin.
The days and things without us.

Cuando dijo su nombre

Cuando oí su relato del exilio
supe que la impiedad no tiene nombre,
y el recio sol caía como un hierro
sobre nosotros, y entendí la muerte.
Cuando dijo, inocente, el hombre es sólo
cero a la izquierda, cero a la esperanza,
movió mi carne un blanco laberinto
de amor, y creció el tiempo de la culpa.
Ciegas palabras en la tarde dieron
su lucha contra el mar, y el sol rodaba
como una purulenta rosa oscura.
Cuando oí su relato del exilio
vino la gran desolación, el luto,
que movía los pasos en la sombra,
y la trampa del sueño, interminable.
Él pronunció su nombre, ya una larga
soledad comenzaba a separarnos.

When he said his name

When I heard the story of his exile
I knew that impiety has no name,
and the harsh sun fell like iron
upon us, and I understood death.
When he said, full of innocence, that man is but
a zero to the left, zero to hope,
my flesh was shaken by love's
white labyrinth, guilt's time arose.
Blind words in the afternoon revealed
his struggle against the sea, and the sun rolled
like a dark festering rose.
When I heard the story of his exile
then came the great desolation, the mourning
that shuffled steps in the shadow,
dreams' endless snare.
He pronounced his name and already a long
solitude had begun to separate us.

El ser no es una fábula

El ser no es una fábula, este sol
que nos mueve en silencio incendia todo.
¿No somos inocentes? Cada sueño
tiene su duro encanto; aquí la lluvia
perdió sus hadas y su blanca sombra,
aquí, a la orilla en que Dios está solo
como destino, en la noche del viento.
Vuelan tardes y frutos, ruedan cuerpos
por la luz en declive, por el agua.
Apenas recordamos la caída
donde la muerte se llenó de pájaros
y alguien gritó que el cielo es imposible.
Pero nosotros no queremos dar
el salto, nos negamos a la dicha.
El ser no es una fábula, se vive
como se cuenta, al fin de las palabras.

Being is not a fable

Being is not a fable, this sun
that moves us in silence burns all.
Are we not innocent? Every dream
has its harsh enchantment; here the rain
has lost its fairies and its white shadow,
here, at the shore on which God stands alone
like fate, in the night of winds.
Afternoons and fruits soar, bodies roll
through the declining light, through the water.
We barely remember the plunge
where death was filled with birds
and where someone shouted heaven's impossible.
But we do not wish to take
the leap, we refuse joy.
Being is not a fable, we live
as we tell, at the edge of words.

Con dura transparencia

Cada esperanza tiene su memoria,
su sol de hierro, su llanto de exilio;
cada esperanza cruza por la muerte
como a través de un túnel desolado;
cada esperanza lucha por nosotros,
nos declara inocentes, nos asombra
de soledad, y en medio de la lluvia
desanuda su ciego laberinto;
cada esperanza llega hasta el poema
que recuerda los trenes y los pájaros;
cada esperanza es un tiempo que dura
soñando, por la tierra inhabitable;
cada esperanza llama por su nombre
las noches y los días, el ser puro
de culpa como un fruto, el hueso insomne
donde el mar confabula, el mar a solas;
cada esperanza cruza por la muerte
con dura transparencia y dura sombra.

With hard transparency

Every hope has its memory,
its iron sun, its weeping in exile;
every hope passes through death
as if through a desolate tunnel;
every hope struggles for us,
declares us innocent, astounds us
with solitude, and in the midst of rain
unbinds its blind labyrinth;
every hope arrives at the poem
reminding us of trains and birds;
every hope is a time that encompasses
its dreaming passage through uninhabitable land;
every hope calls by its name
the nights and days, guilt's pure fruit-
-like being, the sleepless bone
where the sea conspires, confabulates,
the sea all on its own;
every hope through death passes
with hard transparency, hard shadow.

Canción para el final

Perdónenos, pero nosotros nunca
sabremos qué decir ni qué cantar.
Tal vez digamos: el mundo es hermoso,
la soledad nos deja menos sueños
y hace claros en tiempo como el agua.
Es todo. ¿Y su decimos que la muerte
responde al paraíso, si cantamos
que vivir es un vuelo de amor, puro,
y no resulta? ¿Y si nada resulta?
Perdónenos, pero nosotros dimos
al polvo nuestros nombres: su caída
nos ilumina y nos quema por dentro.
¿Somos? ¿Pertenecemos al olvido?
¿Hay dureza en los huesos y los días?
Entregamos la paz, la estrella, el aire
a cambio de esta nada repentina.

A song for the end

Forgive us, but we will never
know what to say nor what to sing.
Perhaps we'll say: the world is beautiful,
loneliness leaves us with fewer dreams
and clarifies in time as does water.
That is all. And if we say that death
is a response to paradise, if we sing
that living is a flight of love, pure,
that does not work? And if nothing works?
Forgive us, but we have given
our names to the dust: its fall
enlightens us and burns us from inside.
Are we? Do we belong to oblivion?
Is there harshness in the bones and in the days?
We give out peace, the star, the air —
for this sudden nothingness a fair exchange.

El mar y los amantes

El mar no reconoce
la voz de los amantes.
Su claridad terrible
golpea, corta, invade
de sucia transparencia
los cuerpos en la tarde.
El mar que nunca vuelve
nos lleva en su oleaje.
Su fruto de hermosura
final, va por el aire
quemando, oscureciendo
la tibieza constante
del mundo en sus orillas.
Tiempo: esperanza: nadie.
(Oh exilio y hundimiento
irrefutable.)
La soledad es esto:
El mar en todas partes.

The sea and the lovers

The sea does not recognize
the voice of lovers.
Its terrible clarity
slams, cuts, overruns
the bodies in the afternoon
with soiled transparency.
The sea that never returns
takes us in its tide.
Its fruit of final loveliness
goes through the air
burning, darkening
the constant tepid warmth
of the world at its shores.
Time: hope: nobody.
(O exile and irrefutable
downfall.)
Solitude is this:
the sea everywhere.

Duration and legend
Duración y leyenda

1972

*Canto y cuento es la poesía.
Se canta una vieja historia,
contando su melodía.*
Antonio Machado

Epitafio del poeta adolescente

Conoció a una muchacha
Bella como la palma del templo de Delos
Cambió su nombre por el de Ulises
Navegante y encantador
Y en las islas innumerables
Apenumbró su corazón la flor del olvido
Lo sorprendió la muerte
Cuando trataba de contar la Odisea

Epitaph of the adolescent poet

He met a young woman
As beautiful as the palm of the temple of Delos
He changed his name and took that of Ulysses
Seafarer and spellbinder
And in innumerable islands
His heart was gloomed by oblivion's flower
Death took him by surprise
When he was trying to tell the Odyssey

Para grabar a la entrada del jardín destruido

Todo esta fue la alondra
Y hoy es polvo
Todo ausencia del laurel y la rosa
Pero si descendieras
Hasta el color o el vuelo
Verías crecer la luna
Las nubes que son otra
De las formas del tiempo

To engrave at the gates of the destroyed garden

All this was lark
And now is dust
All absence of laurel and rose
But were you to descend
To the colour or the flight
You would see the moon's growth
Clouds one of many
Shapes where time goes

Paraíso perdido para el poeta

Nadie puede cantar
Ésa es la tarde
Ésa la luna
Que nos pertenece
Decimos la palabra
Y hay un tiempo
Como el olvido
Y una historia trunca
(Torna rosa mortal)
¿Es nuestra el canto
Durable en su leyenda?
Nadie puede
Merecer esa tarde
O esa luna

A poet's paradise lost

No one can sing
This is the afternoon
This the moon
That belongs to us
We say the word
And there is a time
Like oblivion
And a truncated tale
(Turn mortal rose)
Is it ours, the song
Enduring in legend?
No one can
Deserve that afternoon
Nor that moon

En la luna que he contado

En la luna que he contado
Leve de nombre y de memoria
En la rosa casi historia
Del jardín imaginado
Todo ilumina en pasado
Todo florece en perdido
Músicas de lo que ha sido
O irrealidad del que cuenta
Blanca luna o rosa cruenta
Contar es ir al olvido

In the moon I have told

In the moon I have related
Light of name and memory
In the rose all but history
Of garden fancy's recreated
All in the past's illuminated
In all that's lost all is in flower
Music of a former hour
Or how unreal the tall tale teller
(White moon or cruel rose's terror)
Walks as he talks towards oblivion's power

Alguien se salva por escuchar el ruiseñor

Digamos que una tarde
El ruiseñor cantó
Sobre esta piedra
Porque al tocarla
El tiempo no nos hiere
No todo es tuyo olvido
Algo nos queda
Entre las ruinas pienso
Que nunca será polvo
Quien vio su vuelo
O escuchó su canto

Someone is saved by listening to the nightingale

Let's say that one evening
The nightingale sang
On this rock
For just by the touch of it
Time does not hurt us
Not everything is yours oblivion
Something remains
Among the ruins I ponder
That he'll never be dust
Who saw its flight
Or heard its song

La alondra y los alacranes

Acuérdate muchacha
Que estás en un lugar de Suramérica
No estamos en Verona
No sentirás el canto de la alondra
Los inventos de Shakespeare
No son para Mauricio Babilonia
Cumple tu historia suramericana
Espérame desnuda
Entre los alacranes
Y olvídate y no olvides
Que el tiempo colecciona mariposas

The lark and the scorpions

You are now somewhere in South America
We're not in Verona
Nor will you hear the larksong
Shakespeare's conceits
Are not for Mauricio Babilonia
Fulfil your South American legend
Naked among the scorpions
Wait for me there
Forget yourself but don't forget
Time goes collecting butterflies

Si se nombra la blancura

Si se nombra la blancura
Deshaciéndose en tu mano
Lo nombrado es ya lejano
Silencio de la escritura
Otoño de su hermosura
La palabra es su partida
Hilo de muerte florida
Que va tejiéndole el fin
Mano que ha sido jardín
Porque se cuenta se olvida

If whiteness is named

If whiteness by a name is termed
In your hand disintegrating
What's named now distantly retreating
Silence of the written word
Beauty now to autumn turned
Word departing and regretting
Thread of a flowery death begetting
That still its end continues weaving
Hand that's been a garden waving
In the telling is the forgetting

Song of a foreigner
Canto del extranjero

1976

*¡Si aprisionaros pudiera el verso
Fantasmas grises, cuando pasáis,
[...]!*
José Asunción Silva

Madrigal

Ni siquiera tus pasos recordados,
ese blanco rumor que te acercaba
por el cielo nocturno,
por la oscura vigilia;

ni siquiera esa música de hoja desprendida,
tu música que amé
como en sueños he amado
las desoladas hojas de la muerte;

ni siquiera la orilla del encanto imposible
que miraban mis ojos.
No sé qué soledades
habitan en tu alma,

no sé que cielo impronunciable.

Madrigal

Not even your remembered steps,
that white rumour that drew you closer
through the nightly sky,
through the dark vigil;

not even that music of fallen leaf,
your music that I loved
as in dreams I have loved
death's leaves, desolate and distraught;

not even the impossible spell's
shoreline my eyes gazed on.
I don't know what solitudes
inhabit your soul,

I don't know what unpronounceable sky.

A la sombra de Violeta

Vi perderse tu rostro por esa niebla en que la música
cesa como un jardín al que el cielo de otoño
le niega ya las flores que inventa la memoria,
y empezar en el aire nocturno su aventura,
donde todo nos ama y nuestro canto
puede entrar a las piedras, a la noche mortal,
como los pasos de la adolescente
al custodiado alcázar de luna y de jacinto.

(Miré cómo te ibas sin dolor hacia un reino de alas
acariciada sombra por hojas que caían,
 ¿de qué árbol
donde aún queda una huella de blancura?)
Vi tus manos quebrarse bajo el peso de las horas de nieve,
tus ojos que querían mirarme, preguntar:
¿Qué caminos son éstos, qué río de violetas me persigue?
¿Quién habla por el sueño que mis párpados
se asombran todavía del rumor de la tarde?

Nadie podrá decirte que tu reino no existe,
que lo que tú soñabas como los valles de la música
no es hoy tu cuerpo mismo, tus ojos que contemplan
la primavera en sueños ahora abierta a una danza.

Nadie podrá negar la dicha que en ti nace
o ese cielo, su claridad tan honda,
donde pasa la muerte solitaria
amado por un tiempo de nardo y maravilla.

Sabes ya que tus manos, tocadas por el polvo
de la ciudad antigua
tienen aún el aire de las hojas de cedro,
la música de un blanco país que te amara en la sombra,
oh tú que descendiste por las calles de nieve
y escribes en mi alma una historia cantable.

To Violeta's shade

I saw your face getting lost in that fog in which music
ceases like a garden which the autumn's sky
denies already the flowers memory invents,
and start in the night air its adventure,
where everything loves us and our song
can penetrate rocks, the mortal night,
like the footsteps of the adolescent girl towards
the guarded palace of the moon and the hyacinth.

(I watched how you departed painless to a kingdom of wings
shadow caressed by falling leaves,
                                    from which tree
where there is still a trace of whiteness?)
I saw your hands break under the weight of snowy hours,
your eyes that wanted to look at me, to ask:
What roads are these, what river of violets haunts me?
Who is talking through the dream so that my eyelids
still wonder at the rumour of the afternoon?

Let no one say that your kingdom does not exist,
that what you dreamt like the music's valleys
is not today your very same body, your eyes that behold
spring in dreams now open for a dance.

Let no one deny the joy that is born in you
or that sky, its clarity so deep,
where solitary death wanders
beloved by a time of marvel, when tuberose flowers.

You already know that your hands, touched by the dust
of the ancient city,
have still the air of the cedar's leaves,
the music of a white country that might love you in the shadow,
O you that descended through the snow-filled streets
and write in my soul a story demanding to be sung.

Ahora te presiento como ademán o lluvia
que a mi lado trajera, junto a ti, la hermosura
para que el tiempo sea más cielo o quien lo habita
y el destino conserve la rosa atroz de pétalos nevados.
Oigo tu voz que cuenta del ciprés y la piedra,
de islas que nadie ha visto
como habla el extranjero que sueña con el mar.

¿Por qué quieres volver?
¿Es que acaso la muerte que floreció en tus pasos
te ha negado la rosa del cántico, y el cielo por ti escrito
ya no tiene las alas del ruiseñor que escucha la doncella perdida?
¿Por qué ahora en alba regresas a esta historia
mortal, de otra en que has sido
nombrada para siempre, cuando mi alma
se extravía o padece desamparada y sola por los huertos de otoño?

¿Acaso, amiga mía, la soledad, el duelo
de jardines insomnes (los que he visto en los ojos
de los agonizantes) te desvelan y sufres
un dolor más amargo?
¿Dónde podrías mirarte si no fuera en la fábula,
si está roto en la sombra el espejo de plata?

(Vagas por un país donde las maravillas
a tu lado persisten y la estación del tiempo
no recuerda en tu mano la luna de los sueños
o el polvo de la luna que una vez soñara.
Por tu tránsito ajena del tiempo y de ti misma,
bajo tu sombra al fin que olvidas y te olvida
esta canción te nombra también aunque imposible,
reconoce tus huellas en la arena de un agua ya celeste.)

Now I forefeel you like a gesture or a rain
that brought to me, at your side, beauty
so that time may be more sky or sky's inhabitant
and fate may preserve the atrocious rose with its snowy petals.
I hear your voice that tells of cypress and stone,
of islands no one has seen,
as the foreigner who speaks dreams of the sea.

Why do you want to come back?
Is it perhaps that the death that blossomed in your steps
has denied you the singing's rose, and the sky written by you
has no longer the wings of the nightingale that the lost damsel listens to?
Why do you return now in the dawn to this deadly
story, from another in which you have been
named forever, when my soul loses itself or suffers
destitute and alone through the autumn's orchards?

Is it perhaps, my dear friend, that the loneliness, the mourning
of sleepless gardens (those I have seen in the eyes
of the dying) keep you awake and you feel
a pain more bitter?
Where could you look for yourself if not in the fable,
if the silver mirror is broken in the shadow?

(You wander through a country where marvels
persist at your side and the season of time
does not remember the moon of the dreams in your hand
or the dust of the moon of one who dreamt once.
By your passage stranger to time and to yourself,
under your shadow that at last you forget and forgets you
this song names you too though impossible,
recognises your footsteps in the sand of a water already turned celestial.)

A Greek Verse for Ophelia & Other Poems

Ama tu muerte como amaste tu vida,
deja que te acompañen los que son de tu misma materia,
de rosa demoniaca y hadas como jazmines de lluvia;
no olvides que la música abre al polvo
las puertas de tu reino
y transforma las piedras en las hojas
de ese árbol que perfuma los bosques
todavía y te devuelve
 los pájaros y frutos que sepultó el invierno
pero que han de vivir, Violeta, si los amas,
si cantas al abismo por terrible que sea.

Ama tu muerte, pero no te acostumbres
a su patio de naves, un mar desconocido.
Podrías venir, mirar las cosas que dejaste,
sola y desamparada muchacha para el duelo,
pero mi mano no te alcanzará:
¿Cómo tocar tu cuerpo de blancuras ocultas
 tus ojos donde un día volaron las gacelas?
¿Cómo sentir tu corazón, su presencia en la tierra?
Violeta, amiga mía, en la tiniebla azul,
 enlutada de un tiempo mágico que no vuelve.

Love your death as you loved your life,
let those who share your matter accompany you,
those of demonic rose and fairies as jasmines of rain;
do not forget that music opens to dust
the doors of your kingdom
and transforms rocks into the leaves
of that tree that scents still the forests
and brings you back
the birds and the fruits that the winter buried
but that must live, Violeta, if you love them,
if you but sing the abyss however terrible it may be.

Love your death but do not get accustomed
to its courtyard of ships, an unknown sea.
You could come, look at the things you left,
lonely and destitute girl for the mourning,
but my hand will not reach you:
How to touch your body of hidden whiteness,
your eyes where one day gazelles flew by?
How to feel your heart, its presence on the earth?
Violeta, my friend, in the blue darkness,
mourned of a magic time that does not come back.

A Greek Verse for Ophelia & Other Poems

Elegía

A mi padre

Quisiera ver la luna
Que ha nevado en sus ojos
Para un dolor o música
Bellos países en el polvo

¿Quién ha visto pasar
El tiempo de las hadas?
Dadle una hoja de cedro
O melodiosa o blanca

Quisiera ver la luna
De nevadas violetas
Sobre este cuerpo solitario
Que un día entró a la niebla

Y me contaba en el idioma
De su lejana Biblos
Donde hay un ánfora que guarda
Una alondra color de vino

Quisiera ver la luna
Callada del que duerme
La soledad de piedra
De esa otra Biblos que es la muerte

¿Quién se ha quedado a solas
Con demonios y hadas?
Aquí estuvo el edén
Sólo hay olvido o fábula

Dadle una hoja de cedro
De rumoroso azul
Para un dolor o cántico
Bella palabra de Venut

Elegy

To my father

I would like to see the moon
That has snowed over his eyes
For a pain or a music
Dust where fair countries lie

Who has seen beyond belief
The fairy time pass by?
Give him a leaf of cedar
Melodious leaf or white

I would like to see the moon
That violets snow as they drift
Covering this solitary body
That one day entered the mist

And who used to tell me in the language
Of his Byblos so faraway
Where an amphora awaits
A wine-dark lark to sing daybreak

I would like to see the moon
The dreamer's moon the silent one
The rocky solitude
The other Byblos that is death's dominion

Who has remained alone
With fairies and demons?
In this place there was Eden
Now only fable or oblivion

Give him a leaf of cedar
Of blue as murmur heard
For a pain or for a tune
Venut's beautiful word

¿De dónde es esta rueca
Mortal? ¿Su vino amargo?
Vuela vuela madeja oscura
Que el polvo pide un dátil blanco

Quisiera ver la luna
Callada del que duerme
La soledad de piedra
De esa otra Biblos que es la muerte

Whence is this wheel mortal,
Spinning? Its wine harsh to the taste?
Fly fly you skein of darkness
The dust requires white fruit of the date

I would like to see the moon
The dreamer's moon the silent one
The rocky solitude
The other Byblos that is death's dominion

Lectura de Omar Khayyam

Vendrá la noche en que esta luna
Ha de buscarme y me hallará
Con la mirada del insomne
Que refleja un cielo mortal

De algún tiempo de maravillas
Me llamarán para que vuelva
Tal vez quien hace esta penumbra
O la que duerme entre violetas

El insomne sabe la historia
Del otro azul de la desdicha
Ah de la noche de esa luna
Mi soledad calla y olvida

Palabras que se lleva el viento
Músicas a punto de otoño
En la tiniebla caen las hojas
Para otro cantico de polvo

Reading of Omar Khayyam

A night will come on which this moon
Will search me out and will find
Me with that sleepless gaze
Which mirrors back a mortal sky

Of a time of marvels they
Summon me to retrace my steps
Perhaps who brings this gloom to be
Or she who sleeps among violets

The insomniac knows well the story
Of that misfortune's other blue
Ah silenced in that moon's light
All my oblivious solitude

Words the wind has carried away
Music right on autumn's cusp
In the mist the leaves are falling
For another tuneful of dust

Canto del extranjero

Penumbra de castillo por el sueño
Torre de Claudia aléjame la ausencia
Penumbra del amor en sombra de agua
Blancura lenta

Dime el secreto de tu voz oculta
La fábula que tejes y destejes
Dormida apenas por la voz del hada
Blanca Penélope

Cómo entrar a tu reino si has cerrado
La puerta del jardín y te vigilas
En tu noche se pierde el extranjero
Blancura de isla

Pero hay alguien que viene por el bosque
De alados ciervos y extranjera luna
Isla de Claudia para tanta pena
Viene en tu busca

Cuento de lo real donde las manos
Abren el fruto que olvidó la muerte
Si un hilo de leyenda es el recuerdo
Bella durmiente

La víspera del tiempo a tus orillas
Tiempo de Claudia aléjame la noche
Cómo entrar a tu reino si clausuras
La blanca torre

Pero hay un caminante en la palabra
Ciega canción que vuela hacia el encanto
Dónde ocultar su voz para tu cuerpo
Nave volando

Nave y castillo es él en tu memoria
El mar de vino príncipe abolido
Cuerpo de Claudia pero al fin ventana
Del paraíso

Song of a foreigner

Twilight of the castle through the dream
Tower of Claudia preserve me from absence
Twilight of love in a shadow of water
Slow in whiteness

Tell me your hidden voice's secret
The fable you thread and you unthread
Soothed barely to sleep by the fairy's voice
White Penelope

How to enter your kingdom if you have shut
The garden door for self-surveillance
In your night the foreigner is lost
Whiteness of island

But there is someone coming through the forest
Of winged deer and foreign moon
Island of Claudia for so much grief
Comes searching for you

Tale of the real where hands open
Death's abandoned forgotten fruit
If a legend's thread remains remembrance
Sleeping beauty

On your shorelines time's eve perches
Claudia's time preserve me from night
How to enter your realm if you seal
Off the white tower

Nonetheless in the word is a walker
Blind song towards enchantment wings
Where to hide his voice for your body
A flying ship

Ship and castle is he in your memory
The sea of wine abolished prince
Body of Claudia but at last on paradise
Opening window

Se pronuncia tu nombre ante las piedras
Te mueve el esplendor y en él derivas
Hacia otro reino y un país te envuelve
La maravilla

¿Qué es esta voz despierta por tu sueño?
¿La historia del jardín que se repite?
¿Dónde tu cuerpo junto a qué penumbra
Vas en declive?

Ya te olvidas Penélope del agua
Bella durmiente de tu luna antigua
Y hacia otra forma vas en el espejo
Perfil de Alicia

Dime el secreto de esta rosa o nunca
Que guardan el león y el unicornio
El extranjero asciende a tu colina
Siempre más solo

Maravilloso cuerpo te deshaces
Y el cielo es tu fluir en lo contado
Sombra de algún azul de quien te sigue
Manos y labios

Los pasos en el alba se repiten
Vuelves a la canción tú misma cantas
Penumbra de castillo en el comienzo
Cuando las hadas

A través de mi mano por tu cauce
Discurre un desolado laberinto
Perdida fábula de amor te llama
Desde el olvido

Y el poeta te nombra sí la múltiple
Penélope o Alicia para siempre
El jardín o el espejo el mar de vino
Claudia que vuelve

Escucha al que desciende por el bosque
De alados ciervos y extranjera luna
Toca tus manos y tu cuerpo eleva
La rosa púrpura

If he utters your name in front of the stones
Your splendour is moved and in it you drift
Towards another realm a country enfolds for you
Miraculous gift

What is this voice awoken by your dream?
Does the garden's story repeat, repeat?
Where is your body next to which shadow
Do you slide to defeat?

You already forget the water's Penelope
Sleeping beauty of ancient moonlight
And to another form you go in the mirror
Profile of Alice

Tell me the secret of this rose or never
Where the lion and the unicorn together stand sentry
The foreigner ascends your hillside
Ever more lonely

Wonderful body you undo yourself
And the sky is you flowing into the telling
Some blue shadow of one who is following
Hands, lips revealing

The steps at dawn repeat, are repeating
You return to the song you yourself utter
Twilight of a castle at the beginning
In the fairies' era

Across my hand in your riverbed
Runs a desolate labyrinth
Lost fable of love summoning
You from oblivion

And the poet names you yes the multiple
Penelope or Alice forever
The garden or mirror the sea of wine
Revenant Claudia

Listen to him who descends through the forest
Of winged deer and moon that's foreign
Who touches your hands and raises the purple
Rose to your body

A Greek Verse for Ophelia & Other Poems

¿De qué país de dónde de qué tiempo
Viene su voz la historia que te canta?
Nave de Claudia acércame a tu orilla
Dile que lo amas

Torre de Claudia aléjale el olvido
Blancura azul la hora de la muerte
Jardín de Claudia como por el cielo
Claudia celeste

Nave y castillo es él en tu memoria
El mar de nuevo príncipe abolido
Cuerpo de Claudia pero al fin ventana
Del paraíso

From what country whence what time
Comes his voice the story he sings you?
Claudia's ship bring me nearer to your shore
Tell him you love him

Tower of Claudia preserve him from oblivion
Whiteness blue the hour of death
Claudia's garden as through the sky
Claudia celestial

Ship and castle is he in your memory
The sea again abolished prince
Body of Claudia but at last on paradise
Opening window

Madrigals of life and death

Madrigales de vida y muerte

1978

"¡Ah de la vida!" … ¿Nadie me responde?
Quevedo

Quiero apenas una canción

Estoy cansado de llamar
a la puerta de los que amo,
mi camino se cubre de violetas
y de sombras perdidas de mi canto.

Se ha ido la estación de la azucena
por la muerte que fue una bella fábula;
ahora nadie me conoce,
todos se alejan de mi alma.

No sé qué camino seguir
ni a quién decirle que me ame,
mis ojos miran la floresta
y estoy cansado y se hace tarde.

Quiero apenas una canción
que me traiga tus manos de hada,
una canción para la vida
bajo esta llama de ciprés tan blanca.

Quiero vivir o morir, lo mismo
me debe ser la muerte que la vida.
¿Quisieras tú decirme la canción
de la esperanza o la desdicha?

Sólo te pido una palabra
y algo del cielo de tu música:
Aguardaré a la sombra de mi otoño
cubierto por las flores y la luna.

Estoy cansado de llamar,
pero nadie me abre sus puertas:
acuérdate de mí en la noche,
azucena de un valle que perdiera.

I want merely a song

I am tired of calling
on those I love or at their door,
my path is covered with violets,
with my song's shadows lost evermore.

The time of lilies has passed away
by the death that was a lovely fable;
now nobody knows me, everyone
shuns my soul as alien.

I don't know what road to follow
nor whom to ask to love me,
my eyes look on the forest,
it's getting late, I'm weary.

I want merely a song to bring me
your fairy hands their touch so light,
a song life-long, life-giving
under this cypress flame so white.

I want to live or die, for me the same
must be death and life.
Would you like to tell me the song
of hope or grief?

I ask from you only a word
and of your music only a sky-shred:
I will bide here my autumn's shadow
with moon and flowers overspread.

I am tired of calling,
but nobody opens any door to me;
remember me in the night, lily
of a valley I may have lost, I may not see.

A Greek Verse for Ophelia & Other Poems

Me pierde la canción que me desvela

¿Quién se ha puesto de veras
a cantar en la noche y a estas horas?
¿Quién ha perdido el sueño
y lo busca en la música o la sombra?

¿Qué dice esa canción entretejida
de ramas de ciprés por la arboleda?
Ay de quien hace su alma de esas hojas,
y de esas hojas hace sus quimeras.

¿De dónde vienes, madrigal, que todo
lo has convertido en encantada pena?
Ay de mí que te escucho en la penumbra,
me pierde la canción que me desvela.

I am lost by the song that keeps me awake

Who has set himself, in truth,
to sing in the night and at these hours?
Who has lost sleep and seeks the sleep
he's lost in music or the shadow's powers?

What words are going through the woods, song
cypress of its branches interweaves?
Woe, who out of those leaves fashions his soul
and forms his chimeras out of those leaves!

Where do you come from, haunting madrigal,
transmuting all to sorrowful enchantment?
Woe to me listening to you in the gloom,
lost by the song that is sleep's banishment!

A Greek Verse for Ophelia & Other Poems

Callar es bello

Callar es bello, a veces,
en la desdicha, cuando el alma
reconoce sus flores
en la muerte encantada;

y oír apenas esa música
de los jardines en desvelo,
mientras caen las hojas
que nos llevan, insomnes, a otro tiempo.

Callar es bello, entonces,
oír el polvo amado
que paso por un cielo innumerable
en la noche mortal o el desencanto.

Nada decir, mirar en sueños
la penumbra del bosque,
como un ala que se abre
desde el azul profundo de sus flores.

Oh tú reinas en la noche,
rosa de paraíso que no vuelves,
déjame oír tu mágico embeleso
por los caminos de la nieve.

Dime, ¿qué azul me guardará en tu cuerpo,
perdido, dime, hay otra forma
de no morir sino es el canto
que se desvela a solas?

Callar es bello en la desdicha
bajo la sombra enajenada,
y esperar a que cierre nuestros ojos
el cielo interminable de las fábulas.

To be quiet is beautiful

To be quiet is beautiful, sometimes,
in sorrow, when the soul
recognises its flowers
in death's enchantment growing;

and the sleepless gardens' music
all but barely hear,
as the leaves fall, sleepless,
bearing us to another time.

To be quiet is beautiful, then,
to hear the loved dust passing
through the sky that's beyond counting
in deadly night or disenchantment.

To say nothing, to gaze in dreams
at the forest's gloom,
like a wing opening
from its flowers' deep blue.

O you that rule in the night,
paradise's unreturning rose,
let me hear your magic enthrallment
along the snowy roads.

Tell me, what blue will guard me in your lost
body, tell me, is there another way
not to die but in the song
that stays alone awake?

To be quiet is beautiful in sorrow
under the estranged shadow,
to wait for the fables' never-ending sky
to close our eyes.

En el jardín profundo

Ya no puedo escucharte
en el jardín profundo,
donde solías empezar un sueño
de naves blancas por el mar oscuro;

hoy pierdo la memoria
de tus labios quemados por la tierra,
y ahora sólo olvido
cubre mis ojos que la muerte esperan.

Ah, si tu voz tornara
por el hilo de leve encantamiento,
si la luna imposible
te dijera las músicas del tiempo.

Nada hay que responda
del ayer de tus pasos
ni la viola de mi alma por los patios de piedra,
ni la pasión del enlutado canto.

In the deep garden

I can no longer hear you
in the garden's depths,
where you would once begin a dream
of dark sea and white vessels;

today I lose the memory
of your lips burned by the earth
and now only oblivion covers
my eyes awaiting death.

O, if your voice could turn
on the thread of a spell so light,
if the impossible moon
would but tell you the music of time.

There is nothing that responds
to your steps' yesterday,
nor my soul's viola through the stony
patios nor the passion of threnody.

En soledad escrito

Sólo, a veces, de noche
tu blancura que reina
aún en los cipreses
o en el patio mortal de lo que sueñas,

dejo en mi corazón
y en soledad escrito
lo que pudo ser nombre
de un tiempo que cantara el paraíso.

Sólo, a veces, presiento
que a los cielos del alma
ya no los teje nadie y son apenas
el polvo de tus fábulas.

In solitude written

Alone, sometimes, at night
your whiteness that is queen
still over every cypress
or deadly courtyard of your dream,

leaves in my heart
and in solitude written
what could have been the name
a song to paradise had given.

Alone, sometimes I sense
that the soul's skies are threaded
now by no one at all, now merely
space for your fables' dust to spread.

A Greek Verse for Ophelia & Other Poems

Azules de otra luna

Desolación al alba
de quien busca en la cámara encantada
las músicas o sueños
del olvido nocturno.

¿Dónde encontrar ahora
tus ojos que de nieve
se cubren, o las flores
que tal vez hoy serían nombres de paraíso?

¿No es ésta la desdicha,
hacer del alma un sueño
como a esas reinas de la muerte, blancas,
que sólo guardan sombras, azules de otra luna?

Blues from another moon

Desolation at dawn
of one who seeks in the enchanted chamber
the music or the dreams
of nightly oblivion.

Where to find now
your snow-covered eyes
or the flowers that today
might be names of paradise?

Is this not misfortune,
to make a dream out of the soul
as those white queens of death
that guard only shadows, blues from another moon?

Escrito para ti, en tu nombre

Pudiera ser que un día
retornaras al tiempo,
cubierta por las flores
que recogiste en el perdido sueño.

Pudiera ser también, Violeta,
siempre en el cantico nombrada,
que me dijeras de la blanca orilla
donde ahora es pasión y amor tu alma.

¿Me contarás en qué país nocturno
cantas para que el cielo se desvele,
o abra sus puertas al dolor del hada
que hila en tu corazón para la muerte?

Pudiera ser que recordaras
escrito para ti, en tu nombre,
aquel madrigal de la vida
que habla de un cuerpo entre las flores.

Written for you, in your name

It may be that one day
you will return to time,
covered with the flowers
you gathered in the lost dream.

It may be also, Violeta,
our canticle's constant invocation,
that you will tell me of the white shore
where your soul is now love and passion.

Will you tell me in what nocturnal land
you sing to keep the sky awake,
or let it open to the fairy's pain
she threads in your heart for death's sake?

It could be that you will remember
written for you, in your name,
that madrigal of life, speaking
of a body among flowers moving or laid.

El que no ha de contar su fábula

¿Por qué esta reina dolorosa
que en la noche de mi alma canta:
Deja los huertos de la vida,
bella es la muerte, cuéntame tu fábula?

¿Por qué este oscuro madrigal
preguntándome siempre: cuándo
dejarás la rueda del tiempo,
torna, torna que te esperamos?

No sé de dónde es esta voz
que me ofrece el olvido de su música,
no sé qué otra palabra
me quiera dar las magias de su luna.

A veces hablo de la vida,
digo que la vida es amarga,
y alguien que no conozco, en sueños,
me vuelve su canción de hojas doradas.

¿Pero qué podría decirte
desde las ruinas? ¿Qué podría
decir quien todo lo ha perdido?
¿Cómo hablarte de mi desdicha?

Si fui feliz ya no lo soy,
ni me recuerda lo pasado,
quisiera callar para siempre
y no volver a la ilusión del canto.

No me dejes mirar tus ojos
ni la madera de tu barca.
Mi vida es esto y nada más,
era una vez, érase mi alma.

Déjame, reina dolorosa,
déjame ser el que no vuelve,
el que no de contar su fábula
sino a las hadas de su muerte.

Who shall not tell his fable

Why this painful queen
singing in my soul's dark night:
Leave life's orchards behind, beautiful
is death, you have a fable to recite?

Why this dark madrigal
asking me always: when will
you forsake the wheel of time,
turn, turn, for we await you still?

I do not know from where is this voice
offering me the oblivion of its music,
I don't know what other word
would want to give me the magic of its moon.

At times I speak of life,
I say that life is bitter, then it seems
someone I don't know, in dreams,
turns their song of golden leaves to me.

But what could I tell you
from the ruins? What could he
say who has lost everything?
How to tell you of my grief?

If I was happy I am not anymore,
nor does the past remember me.
I would like to be forever silent
and never return to the song's illusive fantasy.

Don't let me look at your eyes,
nor at your frail wood vessel.
My life is this and nothing more,
Once upon a time, once there was my soul.

Let me, painful queen,
let me be who shall not return,
who shall not tell his fable
but only for his own death's fairies to discern.

A Greek Verse for Ophelia & Other Poems

Preludes
Preludios

1980

A thing of beauty is a joy for ever
John Keats

Elegía

Nada tiene esa azul
para darte la dicha,
nada esos árboles donde habitan
princesas que no son de la tierra.

Escuchas una sonata de Mozart, y piensas
que sólo el sufrimiento redime,
pero no has mirado tu corazón
entre un bosque de lirios.

Nada tiene esa luz con sonido de rama antigua,
con tristeza de pájaro caído en la nieve,
que pueda entre sus mallas purificarte,
darle a tu vida un tiempo amoroso.

Sabes que ya has perdido,
y aún conservas la esperanza, un vuelo;
¿de dónde te viene ese poder
que miras cara a cara a la muerte?

Buscas tu canto, el amor que te salve,
infatigable en tu ascenso por reinos de la aurora,
nada tiene ese azul y nada encuentras
si no es un cuerpo abandonado entre nubes.

Elegy

Nothing has that blue
to give you joy,
nothing those trees where dwell
princesses not from the earth.

You listen to a Mozart sonata, and you think
only suffering redeems,
but you haven't looked at your heart
among a forest of lilies.

Nothing has that light with sound of ancient branch,
with sadness of bird fallen in the snow,
that can purify you between its meshes,
allow your life a loving time.

You know you have already lost,
and you still keep hope, a flight;
where do you get that power from
to look death in the face?

You search for your song, the love to save you,
tireless in its ascent through realms of dawn,
nothing has that blue and nothing do you find
but for a body forsaken among clouds.

Quizá todo ha pasado

Quizá todo ha pasado
y ya nada hay que hacer,
quizá toda la nieve ha caído
y la primavera también es ceniza.

Tal vez nunca se oigan
estas palabras, su rumor
que viene desde adentro
con pájaros o nubes y hojas secas.

Pero mis ojos buscan y hallan
lo que no tiene nombre, lo que nace
de una mano celeste, o miran
un cuerpo dorado con asombro, unas flores.

Posiblemente se ha perdido
el gozo de vivir un día más,
pero hay algo que no conocemos
y espera nuestra canción en el alba.

Entonces un secreto,
la verdad que es el amor, su belleza,
quiera posiblemente darnos
para la muerte su más hondo cielo.

Perhaps everything has passed

Perhaps everything has passed
and there is nothing left to do,
perhaps all the snow has fallen
and the spring is also ash.

Perhaps they will never be heard
these words, their rumour
that comes from inside
with birds or clouds and dry leaves.

But my eyes look and find
what has no name, what is born
from a celestial hand, or behold
a golden body with wonder, some flowers.

Possibly it has been lost
the delight of living one more day
but there is something we do not know
and it waits for our song in the dawn.

Then a secret,
the truth that is love, its beauty,
may possibly want to give us
for death its deepest sky.

Quien ama la penumbra melodiosa

La desdicha me acerca a mi destino
y a mi naturaleza verdadera,
la desdicha, que hace fantasía y palabras
del telar rumoroso de la vida.

Esperanzas no tengo si no es en la leyenda,
vive el poeta a solas y su canto es su cielo.
Quien ama la penumbra melodiosa
despertará del polvo entre alaa y violetas.

Por eso hoy quiero estar tan sólo como nunca
y ver las maravillas de la muerte:
Afuera hay un jardín y alguien, en sueños,
me da un ramo de flores y se aleja cantando.

Who loves the melodious gloom

Sorrow draws me nearer to my fate
and draws me nearer to my nature's truth,
sorrow, that makes fantasy and words
out of life's ceaseless, whirring loom.

Hopes I have not if not in legend
the poet lives alone, his song's his heaven.
Who loves the twilight, its melodious gloom,
will wake from dust amongst wings and violets.

That's why today I want to be as much alone
as I will ever be, behold death's marvels:
Outside there's a garden, someone, in dreams,
gives me a flower garland and departs singing.

La culpa

¿Quién te aleja del valle imaginario,
o te llama con músicas de la esfera celeste?
¿Quién recubre tu cuerpo de hojas moradas,
transparencia que nuestro amor abandonas?

Sólo días fugaces en la tierra estuviste,
en el oscuro azul, haciendo que la dicha
volara en nuestras alma, oh ala sin sombra
de las naves perdidas en la muerte.

¿No puede el hombre ser feliz? Por un designio
escrito en su memoria, lo dorado del tiempo
se mueve en la ceniza y aparecen la culpa
y la caída, pues todo edén es transitorio.

Por eso, en vano recorremos países sin nombre,
bosques plateados del atardecer, buscando
como el amante en soledad, el embeleso
de un cuerpo bello dócil a los labios y el alma.

Guilt

Who draws you away from the imaginary valley,
or calls you with music from the celestial sphere?
Who covers your body with purple leaves all over,
transparency that you, with all our love, give over?

Only fleeting days on earth you had,
in the dark blue, causing joy
to fly in our souls, o shadowless wing
of the ships lost at sea in death.

Can man not be happy? By a design
inscribed in his memory, time's golden measure
stirs around in ashes and guilt emerges
and the Fall, for all Eden is transitory.

That is why in vain we wander through nameless countries,
sunset's silver forests, searching
as the lover in solitude searches for a body's beautiful thrall,
docile to the lips, docile to the soul.

Aventurarse en el pasado

En el huerto, donde los pájaros son el alma,
caen los días, vencidos por el gris, y un canto
que aún recuerda el paraíso, transcurre
como los ojos de nuestras amadas por el atardecer.

Todo pasado es bello y habla una lengua desconocida,
la fuente nos dice historias lejanas,
o la hoja seca entre las páginas de un libro
nos lleva de la mano hasta su árbol de fábulas.

También la muerte se hace bella en un rostro,
y oímos su rumor que nos fascina, su oleaje,
pero ¿no los recubre un polvo antiguo como el cielo,
un polvo mágico del que no se puede escapar?

Entonces, ¿a qué aventurarnos por regiones doradas,
a qué la búsqueda de un paraíso inútil?
¿Qué pasos en el jardín pueden reemplazar a la vida,
la vida que nos llama día a día a su ronda?

Aventurarse en el pasado como buscador de tesoros,
con una canción para despertar a los que fueron:
Oh tú que vigilas el puerto donde están los seres perdidos,
no permitas que nuestra barca se acerque.

To venture into the past

In the orchard where the birds are the soul
the days fall, defeated by greyness, and a song
that still reminds us of paradise drifts by
through sunset as the eyes of our beloveds.

All that is past is beautiful and speaks an unknown language,
the fountain tells us faraway stories,
or the dry leaf between the pages of a book
leads us by the hand up to its tree of fables.

Even death becomes beautiful in a face,
and we hear its mesmerising rumour, hear its tide,
but is it not covered by a dust as ancient as the sky,
a magic dust which no one can escape?

So, why should we venture through golden regions,
why look for a useless paradise?
What steps in the garden can fill in for life,
the life that calls us day by day to its round?

To venture into the past as a treasure hunter,
with a song to awaken those that went before us:
O you who watch the port where the lost beings are,
do not allow our vessel to approach.

Para hacerte a la música

Necesitas de todo, de los caminos grises,
de las hondas penumbras
o las luces del alba,
de pájaros que cantan aún en el silencio;

necesitas del cielo
y la hoja de otoño,
de unas manos vacías o el amor que no vuelve,
de la blancura de la nieve;

necesitas de todo para el sueño,
para hacerte a la música de los azules más distantes,
para que al fin tu alma
tenga confianza en la muerte.

To become one with music

You are in need of everything:
grey roads,
deep glooms,
birds that sing even in silence;
the sky,
an autumn leaf,
hands empty,
love unreturning,
snow's whiteness;
dawn lights,
you are in need of everything the dream requires,
to become one with the music
of the most faraway blues
so that eventually your soul
will have confidence in death.

Primera maravilla

Miro el jardín, los niños juegan
a la ronda, el almendro de corteza blanca y dorada
les da su reino, y todos saben
que están en el umbral del paraíso.

Nada inquieta esos ojos abiertos
a la primera maravilla del mundo,
nada detiene el vuelo
desvanecido en músicas y nubes.

Sólo mis ojos guardan
dolor y muerte – sólo la miseria del tiempo
convierte en polvo la ronda que amamos –
y no hallan paz en lo bello del canto.

First wonder

I look at the garden, the children play
the round, the almond, bark white and gold,
grants them his kingdom, and all know
they are on paradise's threshold.

Nothing troubles those eyes, open
to the world's first wonder,
nothing prevents the swooning
flight among music and clouds.

Only my eyes keep guard
on pain and death – only time's sorrow
turns our loved round to dust – and can't
find peace in beauty of song, chant or dance.

Death of Merlin
Muerte de Merlín

1985

Non domandarci la formula che mondi possa aprirti
Eugenio Montale

Insomnio

El canto de un grillo en el jardín
trae consigo la rama del insomnio,
como un pito de vidrio
que convoca las alas del invierno.

Nunca estuve tan cerca de la muerte,
nunca supe que detrás de la música
pudiera haber el cielo adverso
perdido entre las zarzas y los robles.

¿La vida es ilusoria entonces,
un huerto miserable
por donde van la ronda de las constelaciones
y el reposo nocturno inalcanzable?

Insomnia

A cricket's singing in the garden
brings on insomnia's searching branch,
as a glass horn or whistle
summoning winter's wings.

Never was I so close to death,
never did I know behind the music
could be an inauspicious sky
lost between brambles and oaks.

Is life then an illusion,
a wretched orchard, shabby back
garden, through which the circling constellations pack,
night's unattainable repose, no peace and no solution?

Canción del que parte

Por la virtud de alba
quieres cambiar tu vida,
y aferrado a la jarcia
partes sin rumbo conocido.

Todo es propicio, los acantilados
y el arrecife duermen,
tan sólo una gaviota espera
sobre el palo mayor de caoba y de luna.

Quizá te aguarden para darte
el amor y la palma del vino
o en la orilla sin nombre,
pescadores vestidos de un luto azul.

Vas solo con tu alma, barajando
canciones y presagios
que hablan del bosque donde la hierba es tenue,
lejos de las desgracia que en ti se confabula.

A tu paso verás las islas
que otorgan el sonido de un caracol,
verás tu casa, el humo
que ya aspiraron otros en la aurora.

Mas, ay, si te detienes,
tal vez allí se acabe tu destino;
¿y quién podrá salvarte,
quién te daría lo que buscas entre hadas?

Duro es partir a la fortuna:
el hombre solo cierra los ojos ante el cielo
y oye su propia historia
si se rompe el encanto.

Pero, si quieres seguir, sigue
con la felicidad entre tu barca,
todo está en su favor, el cielo, la lejanía que se abre
con el amor, como la muerte.

Song of the departing

By dawn's virtue
you want to change your life,
and clinging to the rigging fast
you depart destination unknown.

Everything is auspicious, the cliffs
and the reefs in slumber,
only a gull hovers above the main
mast of mahogany and moon.

Perhaps they will wait to give you
the love and palm of wine
or, on the nameless shore, fishermen
dressed in blue for mourning.

You wander alone with your soul, shuffling
songs and omens that speak
of the forest where the grass's touch is light,
away from the misfortune that in you is breeding.

On your way you will see islands
that give off seashell sounds,
you will see your home, the smoke
that others have already inhaled at sunrise.

But, oh, if you stop perhaps
there will your fate end;
and who will be able to save you,
who give you what you seek among the fairies?

It is hard to depart at fortune's whim;
the lonely man closes his eyes before the heavens
and hears his own story
should the spell perchance be broken.

But should you wish to follow, follow
with felicity in your vessel,
everything is in your favour, the sky, the distance opened
by love, as well as death.

A Greek Verse for Ophelia & Other Poems

Por la vida desesperada

No es el azul del cielo
lo que resquebraja la vida,
ni este color del huerto
encendido por las alas más graves.

Sabemos que hay un abismo
que tiene su fuente en los ojos
de quien, perdido, mira una barca
que no tocará las arenas plateadas.

Si existe la memoria
de un mundo grávido de pomas y de música
sólo lo teje la fantasía
por la vida desesperada.

Nadie nos hable entonces de un aire que transcurre,
nadie nos diga que en el principio hubo un jardín:
Sólo tenemos la certeza
del girasol quemado por la luna.

Through the desperate life

It is not the blue of the sky
that shatters life,
nor this orchard colour
kindled by the gravest wings.

We know that there is an abyss
that has its fountain in the eyes
of one who, lost, beholds a ship
never to touch the silver sands.

If remembrance of a world
gravid with fruits and music exists
it is only woven by fantasy
through the desperate life.

Let no one speak then of an elapsing air,
let no one tell us that at the beginning there was a garden:
We possess only the certainty
of the sunflower burnt by the moon.

Del color de otra orilla

La soledad es tu mayor tesoro;
por ella va tu fantasía
constelada de historias,
de mares que se alejan y de blancos países.

Nada podrá, si quieres,
quitarte ese llamado de músicas,
todo es tuyo a su sombra
como el fruto que se abre a otros azules.

Aún la mano del amor
prepara en ella su vuelo nocturno,
y un aire suelta la constelación diminuta
de su crisálida, raíz de la vida y la muerte.

¿No es el rumor entre lirios profundos
del río ya durable por sus fábulas,
la lanzadera que hace al cielo
como un tejido para nuestra vigilia?

Su luz, que ofrece las almenas
a todo lo increado, te hablará cuando partas
del color de otra orilla
como si despertaras en un cuento y lo contaras.

Of the colour of another shore

Solitude is your greatest treasure;
through her roams your fantasy,
constellated with stories,
seas distancing, white countries.

Nothing can, if you want,
rid you of that call of music,
everything is yours in its shade
as the fruit opening to other blues.

Even the hand of love
in her prepares her nightly flight
and an air triggers the tiny constellation
of its chrysalis, root of death and life.

Is not the rumour among deep lilies
of the river durable by its fables,
the shuttle that makes the sky
as a tapestry for our vigil?

Its light, that offers battlements to all yet
uncreated, will tell you on your going
of the colour of another shore
as if, waking in a story, you then told it.

Puerto

El puerto, corroído por el salitre,
conserva las sombras de la desesperanza;
flores no hay, sólo algas miserables
perdido ya el perfume del fondo marino.

Todo esto fue la anunciación
de un tiempo en que los hombres iban
en busca de los abismos cantores
para redimirse de la pena del cielo.

Continuamente se oye el viento
silbar entre las piedras,
y alguien cuelga una red en su puerta
protegiéndose de la muerte que avanza.

El puerto ha resistido
los aletazos de gaviotas insomnes;
quién sabe hasta cuándo, por el don de la memoria,
persistiremos en hallar una estrella.

Port

The port, corroded by saltpetre,
preserves the shadows of despair;
there are no flowers, only miserable seaweed
now that the scent of the seabed has been lost.

All this was the annunciation
of a time in which men went
in search of the singing abysses
to redeem themselves from heaven's penalty.

You hear the wind incessantly
whistling between the rocks,
and someone hangs a net over their door
to shelter themselves from death's advance.

The port has resisted
the flapping of sleepless gulls;
who knows how long, by the gift of remembrance,
we will have persisted in seeking out a star.

La ronda de la vida

Entre los árboles el viento
de tempestad augura
un nuevo color para la tarde,
casi imposible como los pasos en el laberinto.
Todos tendremos que salir a su ronda.
Nuestra mirada en el color sin nombre
verá, sin que la ceniza la nuble,
el fondo de la vida, como en la rosa blanca
los otros movimientos del destino.

The round of life

In between the trees
the tempest wind augurs
a new colour for the afternoon,
almost impossible as steps in the labyrinth.
We all shall have to go out to the round.
Our gaze in the nameless colour
will see, without ash clouding it,
the bottom of life, as in the white rose
fate's other movements.

Gris deseante

Todo el azul perdido, un gris deseante
habita en su rumor,
nadie lo sabe, sólo mi nostalgia
entre el jardín, joya temible.

¿No será el premio que la muerte
me otorga por tanto reino dilapidado?
¿O acaso es el impenetrable castigo
por no creer en la danza de lo que vuelve?

Wishing grey

All blue lost, a wishing grey
dwells in its rumour,
nobody knows, only my nostalgia
among the garden, a fearsome jewel.

Shall it be the prize that death
grants me for so much squandered kingdom?
Or perhaps is it the impenetrable punishment
for disbelieving in the dance of the returning?

Joya abolida para el alma

No todo está perdido, piensas,
aguijoneado por el impulso de una redención,
aún es tiempo de que renazca
el árbol sacrificado por el verano.

Así pasas la vida, la fortuna,
imaginando el azul y el mar por ti cantado,
miras la noche que transcurre
sin una blancura, joya abolida para el alma.

¿Dónde lo verdadero entonces, dónde
la rosa revelada por un sombrío arrepentimiento?
Tal vez no todo sea falso, quizá tenga
ese color que dura después de la muerte.

An abolished jewel for the soul

Not everything is lost, you think,
needled by the impulse for redemption,
there is still time for the sacrificed tree
to be reborn by the summer.

Thus you go through life, through fortune,
imagining the blue and the sea sung by you,
you behold the night that passes
without a single whiteness, an abolished jewel for the soul.

Where lies the truth then, where
the rose revealed by a sombre regret?
Perhaps not everything is false, perhaps it has
that colour that lingers after death.

Canción del exiliado

Quiero tornar a Biblos,
a la ciudad de lapislázuli,
para ser la fortuna
entre los tamarindos y la parra.

Jamás el cielo ha sido
tan imposible, nunca
quemado fue por girasoles
y la lluvia de arena.

Tenía yo esa luz, recinto
que preside las naves como una máscara de proa,
tenía los delfines de piel lunada
y el durazno del fondo que nadie ha visto.

Entonces, ya no puedo
vivir en la desesperanza
en este pozo en que me sepultaron
sin mi túnica de jeroglíficos y pájaros.

Quiero tornar a Biblos,
a la ciudad de lapislázuli,
lo demás ya no importa
si amo entre sus calles el mar color de vino.

Song of the exiled

I want to return to Byblos,
to the lapis lazuli city,
to be one with fortune
amongst the tamarinds and vine.

Never has the sky been
so impossible, never has it been
burnt by the sunflowers
and the sand rain.

I had that light, precinct
presiding over ships as figurehead,
I had dolphins, skin patched with moonlight,
and in the depths the peach no one has seen.

So, I cannot live
in despair anymore
in this well in which I have been buried
without my birds-and-hieroglyphics tunic.

I want to return to Byblos,
to the lapis lazuli city;
everything else does not matter anymore
if I can love among its streets the wine-coloured sea.

Nada perdura en la memoria

Nos persigue una luz
que aún no se decide,
una premura de algo
como el don de la muerte.

Nada sabemos ya
de lo que fuera nuestro,
hace un instante lo tuvimos todo
como una vez, así como en los cuentos.

Y así también perdimos
el aire más profundo, desde entonces
a nuestra casa entramos
a la luz de una vela.

De la antigua floresta
nada perdura en la memoria,
ni aquel rumor que iba
de nuestros labios al asombro lunar.

Nothing lasts in memory

We are chased by a light
that has yet to decide itself,
a haste of something
as the gift of death.

We know nothing now
of what was ours formerly,
a moment ago we had everything
as once, as it is in stories.

And thus we have lost as well
the deepest air, since
we enter our house
only by candlelight.

Of the ancient wilderness
nothing lasts in memory,
not even that murmur
from our lips to lunar wonder.

Lectura de William Blake

Estoy feliz, a pesar de la muerte
que me acecha desde las araucarias,
mi alegría proviene de otro cielo
donde los pájaros adoran la mirada del tigre.

Tigre, tigre, quemante joya
en las florestas de la noche,
¿qué hada se ha posado en tus ojos,
qué jardín en tu piel de luna manchada?

Estoy feliz, aunque la ruina
amenace las puertas de mi casa;
nadie podría detenerme, nadie
que no tenga el secreto de mis palabras.

Reading of William Blake

I am happy, in spite of the death
that haunts me from the araucarias,
my joy comes from another heaven
where birds adore the tiger's gaze.

Tiger, tiger, burning jewel
in the jungle of the night,
what fairy has perched in your eyes,
what garden in your skin moon-tarnished?

I am happy, even though ruin
threatens the threshold of my home;
no one shall be able to stop me, no one
that my words' secret does not own.

Metamorfosis del jardín

Del jardín en verano
nos queda la ceniza,
apenas ese abismo
desde donde no vemos sino tréboles blancos.

A pesar de la muerte
alguien canta a un país desconocido,
acaso sea su duelo la ventura,
aquel destino que nos fuera negado.

Todo es ya polvo en nuestras manos,
canción: no busques ya ni esperes;
tengamos la libélula
y no soñemos la estación que dura.

El jardín sin escalas
guarda bienes y males,
mas, ¿no había aquí una primavera,
un cuerpo que pasaba entre los árboles?

Metamorphoses of the garden

Of the garden in summer
we are left with ash,
merely that abyss
from where we behold white clovers, nothing other.

In death's despite,
someone to an unknown country lifts his song,
fortune perhaps may be his grieving,
that fate to us denied.

Everything in our hands is already dust,
song: cease waiting, cease seeking;
let us hold the dragonfly fast
and cease to dream the lasting season.

The garden without scales
keeps things good and evil,
but was there not here a spring,
a body that passed between the trees?

A Greek Verse for Ophelia & Other Poems

Entre árboles

Si eres tú la que busco
ven en la noche de perdidos reflejos,
si eres el cuerpo amado
ven entre árboles, entre canciones.

Aquí te espera un tiempo
desposeído de sus fábulas,
un cuerpo castigado por la vida
y las zarzas de los caminos.

Si eres tú la que viene
déjame una señal entre los árboles:
un velo blanco, una huella en el polvo
me bastarán en mi miseria.

Ven que la muerte espera,
como floresta magnífica espera la muerte;
si eres tú la que busco
ven protegida por un cielo.

In between trees

If you are who I look for, come
in the night of lost reflections,
if you are the beloved body,
come in between trees, in between songs.

Here awaits you a time
dispossessed of fables,
a body punished by life
and the roads' brambles.

If you are she who comes,
leave me a sign in between trees:
a white veil, a trace in the dust
will suffice in my wretchedness.

Come now that death awaits
as marvellous forest awaits death;
if you are who I look for,
come under the sky's protection.

A Greek Verse for Ophelia & Other Poems

Muerte de Merlín

Entre bosques el reino ha concluido.
No tiene sino puertas con herrumbre.
El sortilegio era falso, los encantadores
yacen bajo el espino blanco.

Sin embargo – para quien pueda ver
a través de sus párpados de escarcha –
existe un rincón desconocido
que brindan la constelación y la rosa.

Aquí el laurel no habita
sino el veneno azulado de la mandrágora,
y el tiempo guarda sus libélulas
para dorar los ojos de los muertos.

Death of Merlin

In between woods the kingdom's at an end.
It offers nothing but dust-corroded doors.
The spell was false, the sorcerers
lie under the white hawthorn.

Nonetheless – for those with eyes
to see through frost-encrusted lids –
there is an unknown corner yielded
by the constellation, by the rose.

Here the laurel does not dwell but
in the mandrake's blue-tinged poison,
and time preserves its dragonflies
for the dead, to gild their eyes.

A garden and a desert
Un jardín y un desierto

1993

Por ínsulas extrañas
San Juan de la Cruz

Pájaro

En el aire
hay un pájaro
muerto;
quién sabe
adónde iba
ni de dónde ha venido.
¿Qué bosques traía,
qué músicas deja,
qué dolores envuelven su cuerpo?
¿En cuál memoria
quedará
como diamante,
como pequeña hoja
de una selva
desconocida?

Pero en el aire
hay un patio
y una pradera,
hay una torre
y una ventana
que no quieren morir
y están prendidos
de su cola
larga de norte a sur.

En el aire
hay un pájaro muerto.
No sabrá de la tierra
ni de esta mancha
que todos llevamos,
de las máscaras
que lapidan,
de los bufones
que hacen del Rey

Bird

In the air
there is a bird
dead;
who knows
where he was going
or where he came from.
What forests was he bringing,
what music does he leave,
what sorrows
cloak
his body?
In which memory
will he remain
as a diamond,
as a small leaf
of a jungle
unknown?

But in the air
there is a yard
and a prairie,
there is a tower
and a window
that do not wish to die
and they cling
to his tail
long from north to south.

In the air
there is a bird dead.
He will not know of the land
nor of this stain
that we all carry,
of the masks
that stone,
of the buffoons
that make of the King

A Greek Verse for Ophelia & Other Poems

un arlequín perdido.
¿Quién lo guarda,
quién lo protege
como si fuera
la mariposa angélica?
Pájaro muerto
entre el cielo y la tierra.

a lost harlequin.
Who guards him,
who protects him
as if he were
the angelic butterfly?
Dead bird
between the sky and land.

Desvanecerse

No tornes, pues el aire
se ha vuelto como rosa de salitre,
y en el muro se abren
oscuros antifaces y arlequines.

La hilandera del puerto
ha cantado a la sombra de los verdes clemones
la canción de las barcas,
la canción de las horas.

¿Tornar? ¿Para qué quieres
tornar? Sólo hallarías entre cofres antiguos
reyes, reinas de traje apolillado:
"Desvanerce, pues, es la ventura de las venturas".

To fade

Do not return, for the air
has turned saltpetre rose
and the wall opens to reveal
dark masks and harlequins.

She who in the harbour spins
has sung in the green clemones' shade,
the song of the boats,
the song of the hours.

Return? Why would you want to
return? In ancient chests
you'd only turn up kings and queens,
monarchs of moth-eaten garments:

"To fade, then, is the fortune of fortunes".

Última canción de Orfeo

Tornas, Eurídice,
a la vida,
debajo del manzano,
y en tus cabellos
de oro y plata
sorbo un licor oscuro.

Quédate, ay, como estabas
en tu jardín, a orillas
del río de la muerte,
y llena
de flores de naranjo
la barca
que un día habrá de llevarme
aguas adentro,
mientras te digo
mi cantilena de polvo
como un perro
que le ladra a la luna.

Orpheus' last song

You turn, Eurydice,
back to life,
under the apple tree,
and in your mane,
gold and silver,
I savour a dark liquor.

Stay, oh, as you were
in your garden, at the rim
of death's river,
and fill
with orange blossoms
the boat
that shall one day take me
out into open waters,
while I sing
my dustful tune
like a dog
barking at the moon.

Piedra blanca

El agua, hasta la orilla,
trae el doliente son de las barcas,
mece ciprés y cedro en cada remo
¿de qué lejanos países habla?

Su rumor, a la sombra
de la palma de vino blanca,
sabe del fin del mundo.
Yo veo mi rostro en su fluir de plata.

No sé si voy en tu memoria
o por la mar ancha y amarga;
vendrá la noche y nunca
podré hallarte en su almena de hojas altas.

El agua se detiene,
golpea la piedra ¿quién la canta?,
¿dónde el patio que daba al puerto?,
¿al cielo de la floresta quién lo guarda?

Estamos solos en la vida
y en la muerte, solos en el jardín y en el alba,
nos rondan animales,
el tigre, el pez espada.

Lo demás es el aire
y el doliente son de las barcas;
"luna, espejo del tiempo",
 oh antigua pesadumbre, oh piedra blanca.

White rock

Close and closer to the shore, the water
brings on the ships, wailing and aching,
cradles cypress and cedar in every oar,
now of what distant countries is it speaking?

Its rumour, in the shadow of
the wine's white palm tree breaking,
knows of the world's end and I see
my face reflected in its silver streaking.

I don't know if your memory carries me,
or else the sea, wide, bitter in its raving;
once night has fallen, I'll never find you when
its lofty, leafy battlements rebuff my grieving.

Water recoiling as it hits the rock,
who sings it, chronicles its fierce behaving?
Where is the patio that gave onto the port? Who guards the sky
that oversees the forest's meshing, weaving?

We are alone in life and death,
alone in garden and dawn, raging
animals prowl patiently around us,
tiger, swordfish besieging.

The rest is air
and the ships' aching, wailing;
"moon, mirror of time", o ancient despair,
o white rock, amidst the long years' wheeling!

Salmo y epigram

Ve al huerto
por almendras
amarillas y rojas,
y a su entrada
canta los nombres del paraíso.
Si Eva
vestida de carnaval
te ofrece una manzana,
sé sabio
en tu pasión
y ofrécele a tu vez
al ángel que, escondido,
espera detrás de la blanca corteza.
Y, nada temas.
Después de todo
sólo son árboles:
un almendro,
un manzano
 que ve con ojos ávidos
desde el muro de piedra el carpintero.

Psalm and epigram

Go to the orchard
to fetch almonds
yellow and red,
and at its entrance
sing the names of paradise.
If Eve
dressed for carnival
offers you an apple,
be wise
in your passion
and offer it in turn
to the angel that, hidden,
behind the white peel waits.
And fear not.
After all
they are only trees:
an almond,
an apple tree
that watches avid-eyed
from the stonewall the carpenter.

Tejido

Si tuviese tus ojos, hilandera,
podría ver lo que jamás he visto:
hilos de plata, hilos de oro, hilos de seda
moviéndose en mis manos
para tejer las cuatro estaciones,
especialmente la primavera
o el otoño que todo lo acaba;
vería el agua correr por la madeja
y torres en el fondo de las barcas,
o miraría en la rueca
las bellas formas que ya son el hilo
en que siempre la muerte nos espera,
el hilo de plata, el hilo de oro, el hilo de seda.

Thread

If, spinner, your two eyes were in my head,
then I could see what I have never seen:
silver threads, gold threads and silk threads,
moving in my hands to spin
all four seasons
but especially spring
or autumn that to all things puts an end;
I would see water run right through the skein
and towers at the bottom of the ships
or in the distaff I would look and watch
beautiful shapes that are already thread
in which, always awaiting, we find death,
silver thread, gold thread and silk thread.

Un verso griego para Ofelia

La tarde en que yo supe de tu muerte
fue la más pura del verano, estaban
los almendros crecidos hasta el cielo,
y el telar se detuvo en el noveno color
del arcoiris. ¿Cómo era
su movimiento por la blanca orilla?
¿Cómo tejió tu vuelo de ese hilo
que daba casi el nombre del destino?

Sólo las nubes en la luz decían
la escritura de todos, la balada
de quien ha visto un reino y otro reino
y se queda en la fábula. Llevaron
tu cuerpo como nieve entre la rama
de polvo que ya ha oído el canto y guarda
la paz del ruiseñor de los sepulcros.

Cerré la verja del jardín, las altas
ventanas del castillo. Apenas quise
dejar que entrara el trovador que hacía
agua y laúd y flor de la madera.
Dijo su canto: el tiempo ha destejido
lo que tejió el Señor, tapiz de plata
que ya sucede y anda por la luna,
tapiz que a la madeja vuelve. Sola
podrás hallar la forma que te espera.

A Greek verse for Ophelia

The afternoon I knew your death –
the summer's purest, the almonds
had grown up to the sky,
and the loom halted in the rainbow's
ninth colour. How, by the white shore, did
her movement go?
How was your flight by that thread woven
which gave almost the name of destiny?

Only the clouds uplifted in the light
told everybody's writing, the ballad
of who has seen a kingdom and
another kingdom and remains
within the fable. They carried
your body, snow between dust branches
that have already heard the song and keep
peace of the nightingale among the tombs.

I shut the garden gates, the
castle's high windows. Indeed I grudged
the troubadour, transmuting wood
to water, flower and lute, entry.
He sang his song; time has unravelled what
the Lord has ravelled, silver tapestry
already happening, moonlit wandering,
yet returning to the skein. Alone
you may find the shape that awaits you.

No sé qué azul de pronto estuvo solo,
no sé cuál bosque dio a la luna amarga
su sortilegio, el girasol hallado
bajo la nave en viajes que recuerdan
las claras aguas del Mediterráneo.
La tarde en que yo supe que te ibas
fue la más pura de la muerte: estabas
en mi memoria hablándome, olvidada
entre las azucenas y en un verso
de San Juan de la Cruz. Qué cielo había,
qué mano hilaba lenta, qué canciones
traían el dolor, la maravilla
que se asombra de ser en esa hora
en que estalló la luna en los almendros
y quemó los jazmines. Tú venías
por el lado del mar donde se oye
una canción, tal vez de alguna ahogada
virgen como tus pasos en la tierra.

Luego te fuiste por mi alma, reina
de fábulas antiguas y de polvo
semejante a las naves que sembraron
de sándalo y de cedro el mar de vino.
Sola te ibas bella y en silencio,
bella como la piedra; había en tu hombro
un violín apagado. Los almendros
del patio y los jazmines anunciaban
una tormenta de verano. El cielo
quebró el espejo de mi casa y honda
sonó la muerte en el aljibe. Estuve
así, perdido en esa zarza ardiente
que en la memoria oculta a los que amamos.
Vestí de luto azul y quedé solo

"en vísperas del día más extenso".

I don't know what blue was, there and then, lonely,
I don't know what forest imparted to
the bitter moon its enchantment, the sunflower found
under the ship on voyages that recall
the Mediterranean clear waters.
The afternoon I knew you
were leaving was death's purest: you
were in my memory talking to me
among the lilies, in some lines by
Saint John of the Cross. What sky was there,
what hand knit slowly, what songs
brought the pain, the marvel
that is awed of being at that hour
in which the moon burst on the almonds
and burned down the jasmines. You came
by the side of the sea from where a song
is heard, perhaps from a drowning
virgin, as your steps on the land.

Then you departed through my soul, you queen
of ancient fables, dust kindred to those ships
that once seeded
from sandalwood and cedar the wine sea.
Alone you travelled, beautiful, in silence,
stone-beautiful; on your shoulder
a violin stopped in its tracks. The almonds in
the courtyard and the jasmines announced
a summer storm. The sky
shattered my house's mirror and death
resounded deep in the cistern. I was
thus, lost in that fiery bramble in which
memory conceals our loved ones.
I wore blue mourning and remained alone

"on the eve of the longest day".

Por ínsulas extrañas

Tuve todo en mi casa,
el cielo y la raíz, la rama oculta
que hace las estaciones
y el vuelo de los pájaros. No había

nada que no viniera hasta mis manos;
pero yo nada quise, y me fui lejos
por caminos, por ínsulas extrañas
en busca de los ojos

del tigre y el rumor
de una fuente
que no era de mi mundo.
En el atardecer lo dejé todo

por una sombra y un alcázar, y hoy
perdido en un amargo
laberinto de hojas,
veo las nubes que se van, la vida.

Amidst strange islands

I had everything at home,
the sky and the root, the hidden branch
the source and making of
seasons and bird flight. There was

nothing that could not make its way to my hands;
but I nothing wanted, and I went far away
by roads, amidst strange islands
in search of the eyes

of the tiger and the murmur
of a fountain
that was not of my world.
In the afternoon I left everything

for a shadow and a castle, and today
lost in a bitter
labyrinth of leaves,
I see the clouds passing by, life.

Imaginary letter
Carta imaginaria

1998

Tú sola, lunar y solar astro fugitivo,
Contemplas perder al hombre su batalla.
Mas tú sola, secreta amante,
Puedes compensarle su derrota con tu delirio
Fernando Charry Lara.

Cuerda de oro

Cada vez que en el huerto
se abren flores, y un ala
que ya ha tocado el cielo,
llega en silencio al fruto y se abandona

al gozo de vivir y a la delicia
de su pulpa; cada vez que en la tarde
viene a mi corazón esta fortuna
de no hallar la muerte,

siento en mí que el Jardín
primordial se hace cuerpo
tuyo en mis labios, y un relámpago
anuda entre tú y yo su cuerda de oro.

String of gold

Every time that in the orchard flowers
open themselves, and a wing that has already
brushed the sky reaches the fruit
in silence, abandons itself to absorption

in the joy of living and the pulp's succulent
delight; every time that in the afternoon
comes to my heart this fortune
of not encountering death,

I feel within me the primordial
Garden becoming your body
in my lips, and a lightning-flash
ties between me and you a string of gold.

Del arte y el destino

INVOCACIÓN

Oh poesía, pájaro prisionero de su canto,
tiempo que huye de sí y a sí mismo se alcanza,
¿perdido está el Edén y es vana la escritura
si el horror de morir no se convierte en fábula?

PLEGARIA

Padre, aparta de mí el cáliz de amargura
que me dan las palabras *pájaro* y *laberinto*,
por el arte de Dédalo en lo desconocido
y por el Minotauro que contempla la luna.

UN VERSO DE PITÁGORAS

Sabia monotonía del arte y el destino,
soñar el mismo sueño e hilar el mismo hilo.
La luna que arde en el celeste brasero
fue un verso de Pitágoras y un ánfora de vino.

TRAMPA DE ORO

Si abres la puerta y hallas
paciendo el animal de ojos babilonios,
no dejes que destroce tu jardín:
las fábulas nos hablan de una trampa de oro.

Of art and fate

INVOCATION

O poetry, bird prisoner of its own song,
time fleeing itself and by its own self caught,
is Eden lost and the scripture vain unless
the horror of dying to fable is transformed?

PRAYER

Keep from me, Father, the chalice of bitter pain
that *bird* and *labyrinth*, these words, provide,
by Daedalus's art, in the unknown contrived,
by the Minotaur's moon-contemplating gaze.

A PYTHAGOREAN VERSE

A wise monotony of art and fate,
to dream the same dream, and through the same thread play.
Once Pythagorean verse, amphora of wine,
now moon in the celestial pit ablaze.

GOLDEN TRAP

If you open the door and find the beast
with its Babylonian eyes outside there grazing,
don't let it turn your garden to waste:
fables speak of a trap that's golden for the baiting.

Grabado en la piedra

Contó que era de Arabia, ese nombre de arena
que dice el cielo estéril cuando es roja la luna.
Vivía siempre al borde de los aljibes, como
si tuviese dos alas para amar el abismo.
Sacerdotisa y triste, cantaba dulcemente
los salmos que entendieron los pájaros y el agua.
Una vez escribió que el tiempo es irreal,
que no es real la memoria; y hay girasoles, dijo,
que sólo son un nombre con una brasa adentro,
que en la noche extremada vino y Aldebarán
son letras que un ángel dice melancolías.
Sus versos los guardaba en un viejo papiro
que tiene aún los límites de un templo. Oh escritura,
bella como las torres de Cordoba y el patio
donde soñó Ben Hazm su brevario encarnado.
No pases sin decirle "te amo", aunque no sepas
quién yace en las palabras de un árabe que olvidan
los jazmines nocturnos, oh doncella, oh perfecta.

Engraved in the stone

She said she was from Arabia, that name of sand
that tells the sky is sterile when the moon is red.
She lived at the edge of the wells, as
if she had two wings to love the abyss.
Priestess and sad, she would sing sweetly
psalms understood by birds and water.
Once she wrote that time is unreal,
that memory is not real; and there are sunflowers, she said,
that are but a name enclosing an ember,
that in the extreme of night wine and Aldebaran
are but letters an angel utters as melancholia.
Her verses she kept in an old papyrus
that shows still a temple's limits. O writing,
beautiful as Córdoba's towers and the courtyard
where Ibn Hazm dreamt his embodied breviary.
Do not go by without saying "I love you" to her, though
unaware who is laid in an Arab's words that forget
the nightly jasmines, O lady, O perfect.

Navegantes

Cubierta de coral y algas marinas
en el fondo reposa
la barca. De las piedras
salen grises moluscos
y tenazas azules y escarlatas.
En ella cuántas veces
vinimos a esta isla de lirios y mandrágoras
en busca de los frutos de la vida,
sin oír que en la puerta de roble alguien cantaba:
solos y oscuros iban los navegantes en la noche,
y era la noche el alba de las secretas maravillas.

Sailors

Covered by reefs and seaweed
rests at the bottom
the boat. From the rocks
spring grey molluscs
and pincers blue and scarlet.
In her how many times
we came to this island of lilies and mandrakes
in search of the fruits of life,
without hearing that in the oak door someone sang:
alone and dark drifted the sailors in the night,
and the night was the dawn of secret marvels.

Oración de los cazadores

> *Tyger! Tyger! burning bright*
> *In the forests of the night*
> William Blake

De la noche que dura
solo queda la brasa de los ojos del tigre;
por ella nos guiamos,
y por ella sentimos su fatal hermosura.

Tal vez, cuando de huida
retornemos al patio que lleva a nuestra casa,
veamos que algo quema los jardínes,
relámpago y pavor su sombra pasa.

No sabemos por qué la vida sigue
y el tiempo nos desvela,
si en la noche una brisa
apaga nuestra vela.

Perdidos, casi ciegos,
no hallamos el solar de nuestra casa.
¿No había aquí un aljibe?
Tenemos sed y el aire nos abrasa.

Oh primavera, herida de la música,
es ya la hora de cristal y hielo;
no nos dejes caer en la noche callada
por la brasa que arde bajo el cielo.

The hunters' prayer

> *Tyger! Tyger! burning bright*
> *In the forests of the night*
> William Blake

Of the night that lingers
only the tiger's eyes remain, their embers;
she is our guide, and through her we feel
his beauty that claws, devours, dismembers.

Perhaps, when in homeward flight,
secure at last we reach our patio,
something, we'll realise, is burning the gardens,
lightning and fear flare in its shadow.

Nor do we know why life goes on,
time fixes us unsleeping,
if in the night our candle
succumbs to the breeze's reaping.

Lost, almost blind,
we cannot find home ground.
Was there not a cistern here?
Thirsty, in scorching air we flounder.

O spring, wounded by music,
now is the crystal hour, the hour of ice;
let us not fall in the night the embers
have incandesced the sky to silence.

A Greek Verse for Ophelia & Other Poems

Ars amandi

Vendrían, si escribieras
otro arte de amar entre las fieras,
los pájaros que cruzan el desierto
a posarse a tu lado
por dos o tres manzanas de tu huerto;
y al llegar a tu casa a tu ángel vieras
- joya aciaga que arde en el aire callado -
venir de lo imposible
a consolar tu duelo.
Sí, pájaros, martirio por el cielo,
ángel en el umbral, puerta temible.
Y vendrían otros bienes y otros males
en la sabia, celeste noche oscura,
a decir que en el arte de las letras finales
es bella la canción y amarga su escritura.

Ars amandi

Across the desert they would glide or dart,
the birds – could you but write another art
of love among wild beasts –
reposing at your side to perch,
two or three of your orchard's apples their rich feasts;
and could you but, once home, for your grieved heart,
espy your angel – quiet air's doomed jewel-torch –
from the impossible emerge
to bring the consolation you desire.
Yes, birds, across the sky martyred wildfire,
the threshold's angel, door and fearsome verge.
And other goods and evils would arrive,
in the dark, wise, celestial night alighting
to say that final letters in their art contrive
a beautiful song but bitter in its writing.

Carta imaginaria
De Ulises a Nausícaa

> *Ulises no puede concluir.*
> *De nuevo en casa tiene que seguir inventando historias.*
> Elias Canetti

Vivo en un reino milenario. El cielo
pasa sobre las torres como un agua
llena de cantos. Puedo ver la luna
que rodea a los pájaros, la piedra
donde alguien escribió que todo es vano,
que el hilo de las túnicas se pierde
y no retorna nunca. Tamarindos
había que en sus hojas anunciaban
un dolor y un música a las reinas
que venían del agua más profunda.
¡Oh almenares celestes y escarlata!
¡Oh velas carmesíes, mástil negro!

Tengo aún en mis manos una rama
plateada sobre la muerte, y una historia
que habla de los que fueron. Las murallas
de la ciudad recuerdan todavía
una nave que estuvo en otra orilla
anclada por el peso de mis viajes
entre sombras, lotófagos, demonios.

Si supieras, Nausícaa, cómo ha sido
mi vida desde entonces: nada grata
para quien vio la flor de los granados
y la esparció en su lecho y su memoria,
mientras cantaba el ciego al que ofrecieron
una silla de cedro y una fábula.

Imaginary letter
From Ulysses to Nausicaa

> *Ulysses cannot conclude.*
> *Back at home he has to keep inventing stories.*
> Elias Canetti

I live in a millenary kingdom. The sky
drifts over the towers as a song-
filled water. I can see the moon
surrounding the birds, the rock
where someone wrote that everything is vain,
that the tunics' thread is lost
and never returns. Tamarinds
there were that in their leaves announced
a pain and a music to the queens
that came in from the deepest water.
O battlements sky blue and scarlet!
O crimson sails, black mast!

I have still in my hands a branch
that death has silvered, and a story
that speaks of those who were. The city
walls remind me even now
of a ship moored on another shore,
one that my travels' weight had anchored,
in amongst shadows, lotus-eaters, demons.

If you knew, Nausicaa, how my life
has been since then: not too pleasant
for one who's seen the pomegranate's flower
and scattered it on his bed and in his memory,
while sang the blind man who was offered
a seat of cedar and a fable.

Tú me guiaste a la ciudad, desnudo,
sólo cubierto por el mar de arena
y por hojas de luz de su hondo prado
para contar mi gloria, mi infortunio.
Te seguí, como dios que me creía,
soñando con mi isla venturosa
donde había dejado tres colores
y un patio y una vid y a mis amigos.
Pero la Reina no esperó mi nave,
la soñó bajo el agua deseada,
y soñó mi esqueleto deslumbrado
por nácares y peces y penumbras
donde cae la tarde y la madera
no es sino puente de un jardín en sombra.

En mi sueño me vi, Rey abatido
por la espada que guardo aún oculta
para el Rey extranjero. Soñé entonces
que moriría lejos de mi patria,
que no volvería a ver en los espjos
las calles de mi Ítaca y el vuelo
que prepara mi arco en esa dicha
perfecta de las olas y las piedras.

Vivo en un reino milenario, es cierto,
sólo un mar de jazmines me rodea.
Salgo a los bosques cuando el cielo teje
la medianoche, solo y en silencio
con mi vida: el destino no me deja
lanzar mi flecha, como yo quisiera,
al corazón del jabalí y la luna:
nunca doy en el blanco, y sólo puedo
pensar en ti Nausícaa. Los feacios
jamás supieron ver en el relato
de Demódoco, el ciego, que tuvieran
en su sala de sándalo al más pobre
y más desencantado navegante.

You led me to the city, naked,
covered only by the sea of sand
and by leaves of light from its deep meadow,
to tell my glory, my misfortune.
I followed you, as the god I believed myself
to be, dreaming of my auspicious island
where I had left three colours,
a courtyard and a vine and friends.
But the Queen did not wait for my ship,
in dreams she desired it underwater,
and she dreamt my skeleton dazzled
by mother-of-pearl, fish and gloomy shadows
where falls the afternoon and the wood
is nothing but a shady garden bridge.

In my dreams I saw myself, King battered
by the sword I keep still hidden
for the foreign King. I dreamt then
that I would die far from my homeland,
that I would not see again in the mirrors
the streets of my Ithaca and the flight
my arching bow prepares in that perfect
bliss of the waves and rocks.

I live in a millenary kingdom, it is true,
only a sea of jasmines now surrounds me.
I go out to the forests when the sky
threads midnight, alone, in silence with
my life: fate will not let me cast
my arrow, as I would want,
straight to the boar's heart and the moon:
I never hit the target, and I can only
think of you, Nausicaa. The Phaeacians
could never learn to see in the tales
of blind Demodocus
that in their sandalwood hall
they had the poorest and most disenchanted seafarer of all.

A Greek Verse for Ophelia & Other Poems

Yo no escuché la historia de mis viajes,
pues veía en tus ojos otra historia,
y esa noche soñé con un vestido
que adoraban tus manos, y una espada.
De lo demás, Nausícaa, no quisiera
acordarme: la nave hecha pedazos,
los marineros muertos y un fantasma
vagando entre los pinos de la isla.
Los pinos de la isla eran tan bellos,
y ya no tengo cerca ni su sombra.
Ítaca fue un jardín, y hoy sólo escucho
cantar a las serpientes; ramas duras,
endrinos y no almendros, y la piedra
donde alguien escribió que todo es vano.

I did not listen to my travels' tale
for in your eyes I saw another story;
that night I dreamt a robe
your hands adored, I dreamt a sword.
Everything else, Nausicaa, I do not wish
to remember: the shattered ship fragmented,
the sailors dead, a ghost
roaming the island's pines.
So beautiful were the island's pines,
and not even their shadow do I have at hand now.
Ithaca was a garden, and today I hear
only the snakes singing; tough branches,
blackthorns, not almonds, and the rock
where someone wrote that everything is vain.

The starless air
El aire sin estrellas

2000

*Soy la lengua de un dios que vendrá
soy el encantador de polvo*
Adonis

Adonaí

Oh Adonaí,
entre tú y yo
no hay hojas
ni desierto,
no hay colores
ni blanco polvo
lunar,
ni llama
que se abisma
en su vigilia.
Oh Adonaí,
entre tú y yo
no hay el cielo estrellado:
sólo
un inextinguible
vacío.

Adonai

O Adonai,
between you and me
there are no leaves,
nor desert,
there are no colours,
nor white lunar
dust,
nor flame
turning to abyss
in its vigil.
O Adonai,
between you and me
there is no starry heaven:
only
an inextinguishable
void.

Cuerpo cantado

Naturaleza tiene
piedad de los colores,
pero no de los cuerpos.
Contempla azules, verdes,
carmesíes, violetas,
y arden el mar, los pájaros,
la luna, las manzanas.
Pero ve un cuerpo, su arco
primaveral, su herida
que llega a ser delirio,
vino del paraíso,
y lo nombra en los patios,
el jardín, los cantares,
y un hondo azul, vacío,
transcurre por su otoño.
Oh estación en que prende
la muerte su brasero.

Sung body

Nature takes
pity on colours,
but not on bodies.
Behold blues and greens,
violets, burgundies,
and burning the sea,
birds, moon and apples.
But a body – here, see! –
primaveral arch, wound
turning delirious, from
paradise its trajectory,
and named in the patios,
the garden, the ballads,
and a deep blue, void, passes
on its autumnal journey.
O season in which death
lights a grill for its finery.

Canción de bodas

Entonces si tuviera
el jardín de tus ojos que está en la profecía,
y el temblor escarlata de tus labios
– fieros relámpagos del paraíso –
no serías la reina de Egipto, oh Dinarzada,
ni yo el esclavo insomne, el perro asirio,
que, encadenado en el umbral de piedra,
escribe para el polvo y ve pasar el Nilo.

Wedding song

Then, if I had
the garden of your eyes that resides in the prophecy,
and the scarlet tremor of your lips
– fiery lightnings of paradise –
you would not be queen of Egypt, O Dinarzad,
nor I the sleepless slave, the Assyrian dog,
that, chained to the stone threshold,
writes for the dust and watches the Nile run by.

Sibila

¿Qué adivinanza tejen
las dunas del desierto?
Reinan la sed y el hambre en los jardines,
y hasta cantan los cuervos.
Ignoras que la vida
se te va, como arena, de las manos.
Acógete al relámpago
que guarda la Sibila.

Sybil

What riddles thread
the dunes of the desert?
Hunger and thirst rule over the gardens,
and even the crows sing.
You ignore that life
is slipping, like sand, through your fingers.
Cling to the lightning
guarding the Sybil.

Un vino triste

> [...] l'aere sanza stele
> "Inferno", III, 23.

Si la noche que cae
sobre el polvo y las flores
fuese tan extremada como el vino
y tejiera otro cántico en su duelo,

saldríamos todos a danzar
 a los claros del bosque,
y cada uno te diría: Señor,
dame a beber por siempre de este cáliz.

Pero no somos dioses, no podemos
vencer nuestra miseria;
nos vamos sin retorno, y a embriagarnos
de un vino triste al aire sin estrellas.

A sad wine

> [...] *l'aere sanza stele*
> "Inferno", III, 23.

If the night that falls
over the dust and the flowers
was as extreme as the wine
and would thread another song in its mourning,

we would all go out to dance
to the clearings of the forest,
and each one would say: Lord,
let me drink forever from this chalice.

But we are not gods, we cannot
vanquish our despair;
we embark with no return, and to be drunk
with a sad wine in the starless air.

A Greek Verse for Ophelia & Other Poems

Visión

Velaba anoche en el jardín
cuando pasó la primavera.
Vi una barca llena de flores.
Eso fue todo.

Mas, sé bien que su vuelo
era y no era de este mundo;
había en ella brasas lunares,
y precipicios de diamante y polvo.

Quizá un día retorne
del reino que he perdido, y en la hora
final cierre mis párpados.
La vi alejarse del jardín,

y en él las hojas, en la noche,
sufren su dolor y su gracia.
Tal vez la primavera guarde
la vida, en su leyenda, cuando pasa.

Vision

I was keeping vigil in the garden last night
when the spring passed.
I saw a barque full of flowers.
That was all.

However, I am well aware that her flight
was and was not of this world;
in her there were lunar embers,
and precipices of diamond and dust.

It may be that she will return one day
from the kingdom I have lost, and that in the final
hour she will close my eyelids.
I saw her drifting away from the garden,

and in it the leaves, in the night,
undergo her grief and her grace.
Perhaps spring still retains
life, in its legend, passing away.

Lunar ember
Brasa lunar

2004

Somos contos contando contos, nada.
Fernando Pessoa

El puerto del almendro

No quisiera volver
al puerto del almendro,
donde hubo una barca de amaranto
mágica y leve.

Volver sería darle
más tiniebla a mis ojos
si todo se me ha ido por el alma
vacía y seca.

Torna a la barca y halla
quien urdió su madera
que es sólo el costillar que han recubierto
coral y perlas.

Ah, de la barca, dice el navegante,
cómo se va y se iba
el áncora que anuda el arrecife;
ah, de mi infancia.

No quisiera volver
al puerto del almendro,
si es ya leyenda el áncora de plata
entre la herrumbre.

Volver sería como
si el aire entre las hojas
apresara un relámpago que hiere
labios y robles.

The almond port

I would not want to return
to the almond port
where once was a ship of amaranth
magical, slender.

To return would be
to impose more darkness on my eyes
if everything's passed through my soul, left
it empty and dry.

Return to the boat and discover
who wove its wood together
for only its ribs have been covered
in coral and pearls.

Ah for the ship, says the seaman,
how it goes and leaves
the anchor that clings to the reef;
ah for my childhood.

I would not want to return
to the almond port
if the silver anchor's already legend
among rusted iron.

To return would be
as if the air between the leaves
clutched a lightning-bolt wounding
lips and oaks.

Diamante

Si pudiera yo darte
la luz que no se ve
en un azul profundo
de peces. Si pudiera
darte una manzana
sin el edén perdido,
un giralsol sin pétalos
ni brújula de luz
que se elevara, ebrio,
al cielo de la tarde;
y esta página en blanco
que pudieras leer
como se lee el más claro
jeroglífico. Si
pudiera darte, como
se canta en bellos versos,
unas "alas sin pájaro",
siempre "un vuelo sin alas",
mi escritura sería,
quizá como el diamante,
piedra de luz sin llama,
paraíso perpetuo.

Diamond

If I could give you
the light unseen
in a deep blue
of fishes. If I could
give you an apple
without a lost Eden,
sunflower without petals
or a compass of light
that rose, drunk,
to the afternoon sky;
and this blank page
you could read
as you read the clearest
hieroglyphic. If
I could give you, as
is sung in beautiful verses,
some "wings without bird",
always "a flight without wings",
my writing would be,
as the diamond perhaps,
stone of light without flame,
perpetual paradise.

Brasa del silencio

Tú, brasa del silencio, que encenizas
todo lo que fue música del bosque,
vuelve a tu nombre carmesí, entre árboles
de frutos y oropéndolas. Qué lejos
el corazón balsámico que daba
la claridad tan lenta de la tarde.
Lo que ya hemos perdido, como un agua
nos ahonda en la rosa que ya no es.
Pasa el fabulador; después vendrá la luna
y se irá con la mano que la hizo de leyendas.
Amaremos la llama del vacío
como una antigua, extinta primavera.

Ember of silence

You, ember of silence, that turn to ash
all that was once the forest's music,
return to your crimson name, in between trees
of fruits and orioles. How far
the heart, balsamic, that lent
the afternoon's slow-moving clarity.
What we've already lost, as water, takes
us deeper into the rose that is no longer.
The fable-maker passes; later will come the moon
and take her leave with the hand that out of legends shaped her.
We will love the flame of the void
like an ancient, extinct spring.

Después será el vacío

Después será el vacío.
Soñemos el minuto de estas flores
para que el tiempo sea como un agua
balsámica y perpetua.

No abramos nuestra casa
al polvo que nos dice lo que fuimos;
más bien como una historia
retornemos al patio y los ciruelos.

Si alcanzamos su fruto
nunca tendremos sed, y en este huerto
volverá la araucaria
a tejer con sus hojas un aire de diamante.

No hay nada como ser
lo que siempre han soñado
los que a la luz del cielo
descubren nuestro aire más profundo.

No calles, que después será el vacío,
su nada, canta ahora
que los dioses te han dado aquel verano
que alguien pedía en su dolor, y espera.

Hereafter the void

Hereafter the void.
Let us dream these flowers' minute
so that time will be as water
soothing, perpetual.

Let us not open our home
to the dust that tells us what we were;
rather, with a story, let us
return to the courtyard, the plum-trees.

If we attain their fruit
we will never be thirsty, and in this orchard
the araucaria will thread once more
a diamond air with its leaves.

There is nothing like being
the dream always dreamt
by those who in the light of the sky
discover our deepest air.

Do not be silent, for the void comes hereafter,
its nothingness sing — now that the gods have granted
you that summer someone requested
in pain — await and attend.

Sonata

La hoja seca del tamarindo se quiebra
bajo el peso de los colores del alba,
así como nosotros podríamos irnos para siempre
persiguiendo el vuelo de un pájaro
a la puerta de entrada de un claro del bosque.
Mas, qué alegría ver en la tarde
palomas de alas plateadas y negras,
sin preguntarnos de dónde vienen,
ni adónde van entre futuros relámpagos.
Qué alegría el delgado misterio
que hay en las cosas casi simples:
en la virtud de este jardín donde te escribo
o en las hojas que caen en el columpio del patio.
Todo esto me da la belleza última
de lo que está a punto de desvanecerse,
como el arco lunar del tamarindo, que se desdora
por el encantamiento de los colores del alba,
como la llama de un violín en tus manos de otoño.

Sonata

The dry leaf of the tamarind shatters
under the weight of dawn's colours,
just like we could go on forever
chasing the flight of a bird
at the entrance of a forest clearing.
But, what joy to see in the afternoon
silver-and-black winged doves,
without wondering where they come from,
nor where in between future lightning flashes are they headed.
What joy there is in the slim mystery
of simple things or things almost so:
in this garden's virtue where I write you
or in the leaves that fall on the courtyard swing.
All this gives me the final clinching beauty
of what is on the verge of vanishing,
like the lunar arch of the tamarind, that withers
because of the enchantment of dawn's colours,
like a violin's flame in your autumnal hands.

Juicio final

No ruegues, que al final te será dado
tu cuerpo, que arde en una rama oscura
en la inclemencia del verano.
Triste belleza inútil
la tuya en ese instante,
cuando te aprestas a volar
como la alondra de la mañana.

Cuerpo tuyo, corrompida joya del alba.

Final judgement

Do not beg, that at the end you shall be given
your body, that burns on the dark branch
in the harshness of the summer.
Sad useless beauty
yours at that instant
when you ready yourself to fly
like the lark in the morning.

Your body, dawn's corrupted jewel.

Monólogo de Sherazada

Ya no quiero palabras, solo un largo
silencio. ¿Entre las ruinas quién decide
contarse y contar a otros? El desierto
nos rodea, las dunas son ardientes.
Todo muere de sed. ¿Quién quiere fábulas?
Mas, hay alguien que dice, ésta es la luna
de las leves almenas, y, a nosotros,
perdidos, nos olvidan
en medio de la perte.
Damos gracias a Dios, y a Sherazada
que recomienza "había una vez un Rey…".

Scheherazade's monologue

I no longer want words, only a long
silence. Amongst the ruins who decides
to tell herself and tell others? The desert
surrounds us, the dunes are burning.
Everything dies of thirst. Who wants fables?
But, there is someone saying, this is the moon
of the slender battlements, and, we,
lost, are forgotten
in the midst of the plague.
Let us thank God, and Scheherazade
who begins anew "Once upon a time there was a King…".

Leaves of the Sybil
Las hojas de la Sibila

2006

Ô saisons, ô chateaux
Quelle âme est sans défauts
Arthur Rimbaud

Polvo y grana

No sabes ya quién eres
pues el aire, que es solo polvo y grana,
te lleva a otra ribera
por una mar de flores amarillas.

Sólo alcanzas tu dicha en los espejos
del costillar raído de los barcos,
entre un viento de vidrio
que corta el duro sol del arrecife.

Sí. Insistes. Mas se cierran
tus párpados, que son un ala tenue
que no ha soñado el palomar del alba
sino las lentas naves de otra orilla.

Y navegas, la dicha es lo posible
que hay en la manzana
del solar: ves la extensa primavera,
su cámara de nardo en la penumbra.

Tal vez, cuando despiertes,
creerás que duermes una noche eterna.
Como eterna es la noche de este aire:
sólo eres polvo, y soledad y grana.

Dust and grass

You no longer know who you are
for the air, that is just dust and grass,
leads you to another riverside
through a sea of yellow flowers.

You can only attain your bliss in the mirrors
of the ships' ragged ribcages,
with a glass wind blowing around you
cutting the reef's harsh sun.

Yes. You insist. But your eyelids
close, which are the faint wing
that has not dreamt the dawn's dovecote
but the slow boats on the other shore.

And you sail on, bliss is the possibility
that may be found in the domain's
apple: you see the vast spring,
its tuberose chamber in the gloom.

Perhaps, when you wake up, you will
believe you dream an eternal night's progress.
As eternal as the night of this air:
you are only dust, solitude and grass.

Cántico de la piedra

También la piedra vuela
y se inclina al misterio:
en ella cantan pájaros
del más profundo abismo.
Entre ramas, oculta,
primaveral florece,
y se abre, dura estrella
y lámpara. No hay muerte
que a su belleza oscura se resista.
Las torres nunca fueron
sino música en piedra edificada.
¡Oh cántico perfecto!
También la piedra sueña
con viejos, dolorosos laberintos.
(La luna es esa piedra que nos guía
en las tinieblas de hoy y las que han sido.)
¿Nada transcurre? ¿Todo está en la piedra?
¿El zafiro, la rosa, la mañana?
En ella el aire escribe
el nombre de los tigres y las hadas.

Canticle of the rock

The rock too flies and
leans over to peer at the mystery:
in it sing birds of
the deepest abyss.
Between branches, hidden,
blossoms primaveral,
and opens up, harsh star
and lamp.
There is no death
can resist its dark beauty.
The towers were never
but music in sculpted rock.
O perfect canticle!
The rock too dreams
of old, painful labyrinths.
(The moon is the rock that guides us
in today's darkness and past darkness.)
Is nothing happening? Is it all in the rock?
The sapphire, the rose, the morning?
In it the air inscribes
names of the tigers and the fairies.

La hora de vivir

La hora de vivir, de tener alas
sobre el abismo, azul oscuro reina
como su cetro de ortigas en el aire
como si te dijeran: Cuida el alma
de tu silencio, que la nada acecha
de cal y piedra viva en lo esperado.
La hora en que es abril el limonero
de tu casa profunda. Busca el hilo
que se teje en los míticos tapices
y no lo sueltes, porque desharías
los dibujos que inventan las estrellas.

The hour of living

The hour of living, of having wings
over the abyss, dark blue reigns
waving its nettle sceptre in the air
as if you were told: Guard the soul
against your silence, for nothingness lurks
in lime and living stone's anticipation.
The hour when April is your deep
home's lemon tree. Look for the thread
woven in the mythical tapestries
and don't let go, because you would undo
the sketches that make up the stars.

No florece la piedra

No florece la piedra
ni el mar florece en los delfines blancos
ni en los corales donde todo duerme.
Calla la noche sola azul, turquí,
sola con un cuchillo entre la piedra,
con un cofre de polvo y un relámpago.

La piedra nos ofrece su ruina y la aceptamos,
¿desde cuándo aceptamos la ruina de aquel árbol
y la antigua acidez de su manzana?
Vamos entre la espuma cardenal,
y hacia el azul marchito
decimos cánticos que nadie oye.

No florece la piedra
ni el nácar ni su luto innumerable.
En el tiempo se calla, se habla en sueños,
y el oráculo, en hojas lo escribe la Sibila.

The rock does not bloom

The rock does not bloom,
nor does the sea throw up a blossom of white dolphins,
nor does it flower in the corals where everything is sleeping.
The night is silent, alone, blue, turquoise,
alone with a knife inside the rock,
with its dust coffer, lightning flash and flicker.

Rock offers us its ruin, we accept.
Since when do we accept the ruin of that tree?
Its apple's ancient acidity?
We head on in between waves,
cardinal scarlet their foaming procession,
towards the withered blue;
as for our songs, there's nobody to hear them.

The rock does not bloom,
nor does the mother-of-pearl, nor its innumerable mourning.
In time it stays silent, spoken of in dreams;
the oracle, in leaves written by the Sybil.

Oropéndola

La oropéndola teje
su nido en lo más alto
del tamarindo.
¿Si anidara en el cielo
sería menos pájaro?

La luz cae sobre ella:
negras alas
no dejan que se vuelva
transparente
como angélica flecha.

Cuando la tarde vuelve
gris y plata las ramas,
su canto
ya desierto
hace que exista el bosque.

La oropéndola,
flor
amarilla en tus manos,
se abandona al soñar.
¡Qué lámpara ilusoria!

Oriole

The oriole weaves
her nest at the
tamarind's zenith.
If she nested in the sky
would she be less a bird?

Light falls over her:
dark wings
keep her from turning
transparent as
an angelic arrow.

When the afternoon turns
the branches grey and silver,
her song
already desert brings
the forest to exist.

The oriole,
yellow
flower between your hands,
abandons herself to dream.
Lamp so illusory!

Simurg

La vida, ese palacio de cristal
que se rompe en el agua,
como si el tiempo fuese
de otra estación: La vida.

¿Nada sabemos? ¿Sólo
que la arena transcurre
como las viejas torres
a punto de ser aire?

Sobre ellas el simurg
deja caer su pluma,
y las piedras resisten
por el laúd que guarda.

Ese palacio de cristal, soñado
de un libro que se escribe,
y escribirá en la lengua
de Adán y de los pájaros.

Zuritas que ya fueron
en la tarde la luna,
y el árbol en que duermen
sus cenizas de plata:

(los árabes conocen su huerto de manzanas.
Quieras tú que encontremos
su antiguo laberinto.)

La vida – es el otoño –
navega en un relámpago.
¡Oh la estación del vino,
oh llama de unos labios!

Simurgh

Life, that palace of crystal
that breaks in the water,
as if time came
from another season: Life.

Do we know nothing? Only
that the sand flows
like ancient towers
about to become air?

Over them the simurgh
lets its feather drop,
and the rocks resist thanks
to the lute's watchfulness.

That palace of crystal, dreamt
by a book being written,
which shall be written in the tongue
of Adam and the birds.

Doves that already were
in the afternoon the moon,
and in the tree where they sleep
its silver ashes:

(the Arabs know well
their apple orchard.
May you wish that we find
their ancient labyrinth).

Life – is the autumn –
sails in a lightning flash.
O the wine's season,
O lips' flame flesh!

No des paz a tu reino

No des paz a tu reino
entre escudos de bronce voladores.
De noche, los geranios
que tocan el alféizar
dejan hojas o lámparas insomnes
color de un tiempo que se va, se ha ido.
(Cantarela del bosque.)
Pero aún hay en ellos
frutos desconocidos de otra hora,
que invaden y nos mienten
con su llama de polvo.

Oh tú que en la penumbra
sueñas tu historia oculta, ve a los cuentos
que aguardan en la vida y en la muerte
como una primavera que huye y nunca pasa,
y sufre la poesía,
tu purgatorio de mortal espino:
No des paz a tu reino
entre escudos de bronce voladores.

Do not give peace to your kingdom

Do not give peace to your kingdom
amid shields of flying bronze.
At night, the geraniums
that brush the windowsill
abandon leaves or sleepless lamps
colour of a time that is leaving, that has left.
(Lullaby of the woods.)
But still they bear
unknown fruits of another time,
that invade and deceive us
with their flame of dust.

O you that in the gloom
dream your hidden history, go to the stories
that await in life and in death
as a spring that flees and never passes,
and suffer poetry,
your purgatory of mortal thorns:
do not give peace to your kingdom
amid shields of flying bronze.

Nocturno

En la tiniebla de coral, en sueños,
y ebrio de pasos y alas nunca oídos,
subo por la escalera
"de púrpuras violetas carmesíes".

¿Quién eres tú que naces
de una fuente que viene de las dunas?
¿Quién te dio mi pasión, mi adivinanza?
¿Quién hizo de mi vida un sueño, un cuento?

Dime, dime tu nombre:
No sé si eres mi vino o mi demonio o mi ángel.
Vuelas por mi lagar,
y no sé de tus remos ni tu nave.

Quizá cuando retorne,
mire yo un regio palomar del alba,
o el color de la piel de los leopardos
que vigilan el huerto innumerable.

Suben por la escalera pasos y alas,
los que saben del tiempo y de su ronda.
Miro el azul cerrado
en estas soledades del alcázar.

Déjame que me sueñe vino oscuro,
deja de ser en mi desierto ese otro
que arde en mí, el extranjero
de labios de cristal y ojos de plata.

Nocturnal

In the coral darkness, in dreams,
and drunk with steps and wings never heard,
I ascend the stairway
"blue and purple and scarlet, of needlework".

Who are you who spring
out of a fountain that comes from the dunes?
Who gave you my passion, my riddle?
Who made of my life a dream, a story?

Tell me, tell me your name:
I do not know if you are my wine, my demon or my angel.
You fly through my winepress
and I am unaware of your oars and your ship.

Perhaps when I return then
will I look at the dawn's regal dovecote,
or the colour of the leopards' skin,
those guarding the innumerable orchard.

Ascend the stairway steps and wings,
who know of time and its round.
I behold the closed blue
in this palace's solitudes.

Let me dream myself a dark wine,
cease to be in my desert that other
who burns in me, the foreigner
crystal-lipped and silver-eyed.

Cuento del paraíso

> *"Jeder Engel ist schrecklich"*
> Rainer Maria Rilke

Viene de la tiniebla, si preguntas,
este rostro quemado por el nácar,
donde quiso el relámpago formarse
para hacer una llama y una perla.
Vi sus alas partidas, que se abrieron
como velas en busca de su puerto.
El salitre y la hiel fueron saetas
al paso de sus reinos voladores
de donde sale el cántico manchado.
Sube de la tiniebla, y está solo
pendiente de tu árbol. ¿No hay ortigas?
Nada puedes hacer: Todo está dicho
si ya todo ha soñado quien esconde
su alma entre el dolor y la floresta.
Viene del viejo azul. El tiempo pasa
y pasan los colores. No hay la dicha
que pudo ser y no será el balsámico
silencio de unos labios de polvo.
Todo es ayer y nada en la memoria
cuando el viajero ya quemó sus naves.
Despiertas con los ojos alunados.
¡Oh braceros: "Todo ángel es terrible"!
Si eres arca sellada de la arcilla
¿quién reveló las letras de tu nombre?

La manzana, coral de un alba oscura,
silba como relámpago en tus labios.

Paradise story

> "*Jeder Engel ist schrecklich*"
> Rainer Maria Rilke

It comes from darkness, if you ask,
this face mother-of-pearl has scorched,
where lightning's impulse was to shape
itself to make a flame and a pearl.
I saw its split wings, opening up
sail-like in searching for their port.
The saltpetre and the gall were arrows
crossing their flying kingdoms' path,
from where a *saeta*'s blemished canticle is born.
It rises out of darkness, and it stands alone
hanging from your tree. Are there no nettles?
There is nothing you can do: everything is said
if everything has been dreamt by one who hides
his soul among the forest and the pain.
Its source is in old blue. Time passes
and colours pass too. The bliss that could have been
is not, nor will it be some lips'
balsamic silence in the dust.
Everything is yesterday and nothing in memory
when the sea-traveller has already burnt his ships.
With lunar eyes you wake.
O labourers, "Every angel is terrifying"!
If you were an ark sealed by clay
who then disclosed the letters of your name?

The apple, a dark dawn's coral,
whistles like lightning between your lips.

The artist of silence
El artista del silencio

2012

Telar con pájaros y hojas

Telar inexorable
con pájaros y hojas,
vuelos y hondos colores
van de su aire a su nada.

La luz ya es un abismo,
y a su diamante el sueño
arde en un laberinto
de amargas soledades,

Tiempo, laúd que tañen
los días cuando pasan.
Telar, la vida es tuya,
perpetua y fugitiva.

Melancolía en el juego
mortal de una extremada
dolencia de las músicas
de los hilos eternos.

Con pájaros y hojas
escrito fue este canto…
Aquí pudo existir el paraíso,
sólo que el paraíso era una sombra.

Loom of birds and leaves

Inexorable loom
of birds and leaves,
flights and deep colours
flow from air to nothingness.

Light is already abyss,
and its diamond dreams
burn in a labyrinth
of bitter solitudes,

time and lute toll
the passing days.
Loom, life is yours,
perpetual and fleeting.

Melancholy in the mortal
game of an extreme
suffering of music
from the eternal threads.

With birds and leaves
was this song written …
Here could paradise have existed,
but that paradise was a shadow.

Invitación

Por el camino estrecho ven,
vuela por la floresta,
adonde vuelve de su propio cielo
la palmera del dátil encarnado,
y a donde el vino que derraman
unos labios de cobre
no lleve las tinieblas, ese aroma
del lirio en que la víbora se enrosca.
Eso escribí, y mi canto fue el principio
del duro encantamiento
del corazón; eso fue todo
cuanto escribí en la arena, viendo los barcos
      que se iban.
Eso fue todo.

Invitation

Come by the narrow road,
fly through the forest,
where the date palm with its rust fruit
returns from its own sky,
and where the wine spilt
by some copper lips
shall not carry darkness, that scent
of lily where the viper lies curled.
That I wrote, and my song was the start
of the heart's hard
enchantment; that was all
that I wrote in the sand, watching the boats
       sail away.
That was all.

Palabras que ya fueron

Si todo ha sido lo de siempre, si
los árboles no son de tamarindo
sino madera gris donde clausuran
su cielo los canarios.
Si en el puerto las naves
son de cristal y abismo:
Historias que nos da el acantilado.
Si en las calles aún
quema la arena roja y amarilla;
si todo es siempre un cuento
que torna y se repite
como el dolor de un ánfora de vino.
Si hay unos labios secos
quemados en el patio
donde hubo un aljibe, el hondo día
nos lleve hasta el profundo
silencio y no halle músicas
cuando en el alba aún es media noche.
¿Vendrá la primavera?
Dadme su flor, el vano sortilegio
que abra esta canción, su oscuro reino.

Words that already were

If everything has been as it always has, if
the trees are not tamarinds
but grey wood where canaries
seal off their sky.
If in the port the ships
are of crystal and abyss:
Histories given us by the cliff.
If in the streets the sand
still burns yellow and red;
if everything is always a story
turning, self-repeating
like a wine jar's pain.
If there are dry lips
burnt in the courtyard
where once was a cistern, let the deep
day lead us to the deep
silence and let it not find music
when the dawn is still midnight.
Will the spring come?
Give me its flower, the vain sorcery
that opens this song, its dark kingdom.

Apariciones

Nada quisiera el canto
de la estación que al cielo quema.
También a la virtud se ha nombrado tiniebla
si hay que morir
y hacerse polvo. ¿Quién
no fue ceniza y torre derribada?
Vanos son los escudos, como alas,
si una copa de vino es suficiente
piedad para el guerrero.
Sí, la embriaguez de todo lo soñado
que al despertar se pierde.
Quizá la vida nos depara
alianzas con ejércitos que fueron;
quizá el desprecio de los dioses sea
crearnos de la arcilla de las apariciones.

Apparitions

Nothing does the season's sky
burning song want.
Virtue also's been named
a murky ignorance
if die we must
and turn to dust. Who
has not been ash, demolished tower?
Vain are shields, like wings,
if for the warrior a cup of wine
is sufficient mercy.
Yes, drunkenness of all that's been dreamt
dissipated in awakening.
Life perhaps puts in our way,
with armies that once were, alliances;
perhaps the gods' contempt is this:
to create us out of apparitions' clay.

Versos del silencio

Nada podrá decirte
quien nada sabe, solo
si la memoria deja de ser sueño
y torna a su raíz de rama y pájaro,
serías página blanca
de alguien que supo amar y fue al silencio,
palabra en que las horas
venían del aire y por el aire iban
a la quietud de un rostro que no tiene
sino abismos y párpados callados.
Nada podrás decirme
si nada sabes, porque sólo hay labios
que fueron un color en el vacío.
Vive, pues, con la ausencia de ti mismo,
con tu viaje a las islas ignoradas,
que si hallas la puerta del espejo
tal vez despiertes en tu purgatorio.

Verses of silence

Nothing could say to you
who nothing knows, only
if memory ceases to be a dream
and returns to its root of branch and bird,
would you be blank page
for someone who could love and went to silence,
words in which the hours
were coming from the air, through the air going
towards the quietude of a face that has
abysses only, silent eyelids.
Nothing could you say to me
if you nothing know, because there are only lips
that once came as colour in the void.
Live, then, in the absence of yourself,
in your voyage to the unknown islands,
that if you find the mirror's door
you may awaken in your purgatory.

La última orilla

Cómo saber si el río va o viene de sí mismo,
o si el agua no es solo un cántico del tiempo.
Ah, cómo hacer que el cedro sembrado en esta barca
florezca en los desiertos de la última orilla.

Tal vez sería una vez si el alba que nos ciega
en la noche enemiga no fuese el puro sueño
de aquél que no se pierde porque, ya vuelto sombra,
mira hundirse en el río los remos florecidos.

The last shore

How then to know if of itself the river comes or goes,
or whether the water's but time's canticle.
Ah, how can we make the cedar planted in this boat
flower in the deserts of the last shore.

Perhaps there was a time in which the dawn that blinds
us in the enemy night was not the pure dream
of one not lost, now already turned shadow,
who watches the flowering oars sink in the river.

El artista del silencio

¿Habría de negarlo?
Si soy el último hombre que camina sobre la tierra
y habría de negarlo si no hay pájaros
que canten una canción en el otoño
si no hay otoños si ya ha pasado el tiempo de las estaciones
y habría de negarlo
si no hay azul a quien decirle mi desconcierto
si estoy donde los colores no tienen nombre
en el juicio final incesante de los jardines
Soy el último hombre que grita sobre la tierra
que grita al cielo que se ha ocultado para siempre
y habría de negarlo a quién ¿a Dios?
acaso Dios es el artista del silencio
de tantas hojas que no son o siguen cayendo al abismo
y estallan en el aire sucio pero en qué aire.

The artist of silence

Should it be denied?
If I am the last man walking on the earth
I would have to deny it
if there are no birds to sing an autumn song
if there is no autumn if the time of the seasons has already passed
I would have to deny it
if there is no blue for me to tell my bewilderment
if I am where the colours have no name
in the gardens' incessant final judgement
I am the last man shouting on the earth
who shouts to the sky that has hidden itself forever
and I would have to deny it to whom, to God?
God is perchance the artist of silence
for there are so many leaves that are not or keep falling into the abyss
and explode in the squalid air but what air.

Abyss unveiled
Abismo revelado

2017

Do not go gentle into that good night
Dylan Thomas

Oración

¿Sólo es real lo que toco en el abismo?
Lo que un día fue soñado
ilumina mis párpados
con un levísimo resplandor, un azul
del bosque entre hojas húmedas.

Voy por la escala de Jacob.
Terrible es la belleza:
demonios hay y ángeles en su delirio alado.
Vivir, morir en sueños.

Música de la memoria, protégeme;
llama de la imaginación
que resucitas, guíame
a tu árbol encarnado de la noche.

Ningún mayor dolor que soñarse de polvo.
Vergine madre, figlia del tuo figlio,
invéntame en la música de mi último duelo
y el resplandor de la hoja
cuando pasa el otoño.

Prayer

Shall only this be real: what I brush in the abyss?
What one day was dreamt
illuminates my eyelids
with the slightest splendour; a blue from
the forest between humid leaves.

I go by Jacob's ladder.
Terrible is beauty:
demons there are and angels in winged delirium.
To live, to die in dreams.

Music of memory, guard me;
imagination's flame
resurgent, guide me
to night's incarnate tree.

No greater pain than to dream oneself of dust.
Vergine madre, figlia del tuo figlio
invent me from my last mourning's music
and the splendour of the leaf
as autumn passes.

Sortilegio

Abierta te hallas a la noche,
y esperas un rumor
que hable de historias
casi invisibles de tan puras, blancas leyendas.

Y así me esperas.
Nada sabes
de mi vida entre cánticos oscuros.
¿Guardas aún el resplandor
que abrió los surcos
y dejó las semillas?
Alondras hay o había.
Aires del cielo, mar callado.

¿Quemo mis naves si me acerco
sin pasos musicales?
Acaso un sortilegio
me tornará puro,
invisible.

Spell

Open you find yourself at night,
awaiting a murmur
that will speak of stories
almost invisible from being such pure, white legends.

And thus you lie in wait.
You know nothing
of my life in between dark canticles.
Do you still keep the radiance
that opened up the furrows
and left behind the seeds?
Larks there are or were.
Airs from the sky, silent sea.

Shall it burn the ships, to approach
music-less in my steps?
Perhaps a spell
will make me pure,
invisible.

De cedro y de ciprés

Soy exiliado:
alguien me dijo que podría ser
un hacedor de fábulas.
Sueño con mi alma, es lo que tengo,
únicamente mi alma:
pura, manchada,
o casi leve como las hojas que están a punto de ser luz
y alzan el vuelo de una rama que aún no existe,
en el vacío más puro.
Como un cuento soñado en la memoria.

Sueño con árboles y en ellos veo mi ceniza:
lo que soy, la nostalgia del futuro.
Mi casa es de ciprés y mi puerta de cedro:
ven mi ángel, mi demonio, entra en mi casa, ¿no podrías
despertarme? Sólo soñándome en tu sueño
quizá vuelto de luz, hoja que vuela por sí misma, pájaro.

En mi principio está mi fin: soy exiliado,
alguien me dijo que podría ser
un hacedor de fábulas.

Of cedar and cypress

I am an exile:
somebody told me I could be
a fable-maker.
I dream my soul, it's all I have,
only my soul:
pure, stained,
or almost as light as leaves about to become light
that spring up to the flight of a branch still to be,
in the purest void.
As a story dreamt in memory.

I dream of trees and in them I see my ash:
what I am, nostalgia for the future.
My house is made of cypress, my door of cedar:
come angel of mine, my demon, enter my home, couldn't
you wake me up? Only dreaming me in your dream
maybe turned to the light, leaf flying on its own, bird.

In my beginning is my end: I am an exile,
somebody told me I could be
a fable-maker.

Abismo revelado

Dureza del camino:
piedras agudas ruedan
como por un acantilado.
Temor celeste que rodean las zarzas.
Quizá ya descendimos
por escaleras de piedra húmeda
a donde hay estrellas repitiéndose
dolorosas de polvo,
como en un círculo perpetuo.

El tiempo quema el vuelo
de las hojas que caen y abre la flor azul.
Abismo revelado:
nuestro único don en lo desconocido.

Abyss unveiled

Harshness of the road:
sharp rocks roll
as down a cliff.
Celestial fear the brambles cluster round.
Perhaps we have already descended
down damp stone stairways
where there are stars repeating themselves
painfully out of dust,
as in a perpetual cycle.

Time burns the flight
of the falling leaves and the blue flower opens up.
Abyss unveiled:
our only gift in the unknown.

Naufragio

Teníamos únicamente
un tamarindo florecido
en el patio del cielo,
y a su sombre
hacíamos barquitos de papel.
Cuando venían las lluvias diluviales
les poníamos nombres maravillosos:
unicornio, castillo de aire,
y los hacíamos navegar
hasta que naufragaban en la luna.

Así vivíamos, soñábamos
en nuestra casa que hoy no está
amurallada de cánticos.
Sólo tenemos la desdicha, el aljibe vacío,
ya no está el tamarindo, sólo cenizas en el patio.
Pero nunca olvidamos
la música de los espejos.

Vinieron en la noche y se llevaron
el solar de las rondas, los trompos, las cometas.
Sólo nos queda el aire que no cesa
y la luna
donde naufragan todavía
barquitos de papel
que van a dar a la mar del patio del cielo.

Shipwreck

We had only
a flowering tamarind
in the sky's courtyard
and in its shadow
we made little paper boats.
When the flooding rains came in
we named them with fantastic names:
unicorn, air castle,
and we made them sail
until they shipwrecked on the moon.

It was thus that we lived, we dreamed
in our home that today is no longer
enclosed within canticle walls.
We have only misfortune, the empty cistern,
gone is the tamarind, only ashes in the courtyard remain.
But we have never forgotten
the mirrors' music.

They came at night and took
the rounds' terrain, the spinning tops, the kites.
We are left only with the unyielding air
and the moon
where paper boats still
find their shipwreck, headed *downward*
to the sea of the sky's courtyard.

Notes

In *Being is not a fable* (*El ser no es una fábula*, 1968)

The epigraph is taken from Paul Valéry's *Le Cimetière marin* ("The Graveyard by the sea"), quoted in French in the original in Spanish and translated as "the sea will always recommence" by David Pollard for Brooklyn Rail InTranslation magazine.

> "a zero to the left, zero to hope" in "When he said his name" (p.38):

It is probable that Quessep is making a play on words with a traditional Colombian saying: "x es un cero a la izquierda" ("x is a zero to the left"), which means that someone or something is nothing, means nothing, has no significance. Other Latin American poets, such as the Peruvian César Vallejo in the XVIth poem of *Trilce*, have used this expression as well.

> "the sea conspires, confabulates" in "With hard transparency" (p.42):

The verb "confabular" is difficult to translate with all the meaning it has in Spanish. It roughly means the same thing as "to conspire" but has an element in Spanish that is not present in that word: "fable" ("fabular" = to fable) – as the title of this first book suggests, this word is very meaningful to Quessep. Therefore "confabular" means to conspire but to conspire by telling a fable, a story, with ("con") someone else.

In *Duration and legend* (*Duración y leyenda,* 1972)

The epigraph is taken from Antonio Machado's *De mi cartera* ("From my wallet"), which can be translated as "Song and tale is poetry./An old tale is sung,/by telling its melody".

"In the moon I have told" (p.56):

This poem is the first of Quessep's published work to have a definite rhyme scheme in its original Spanish: the poem is structured in the manner of a "Décima Espinela", that is to say, a stanza of ten lines that has a ABBAACCDDC pattern. It was named thus in honour of Vicente Espinel, a poet, priest and musician of the Spanish Golden Age who is considered to be the first to use and perfect this poetic technique. Fortunately, we have been able to preserve its rhyming pattern in translation.

"Mauricio Babilonia" in "The lark and the scorpions" (p.60):

Mauricio Babilonia is a literary character who makes a brief but fundamental appearance in Gabriel Garcia Márquez's *One Hundred Years of Solitude*. He is a mechanic born and raised in Macondo who works for the American banana company and later becomes Meme's lover, in spite of her mother's disapproval of their love in view of his socio-economic origins. His presence was famously accompanied by a cloud of yellow butterflies and he is also the father of Aureliano Babilonia, the character that closes the book. His appearance in the novel is brought to an end when he is shot in the back at the moment he is sneaking behind the house to attend his daily erotic encounters with Meme. Garcia Márquez describes this episode in the following terms: "That night the guard brought down Mauricio Babilonia as he was lifting up the tiles to get into the bathroom where Meme was waiting for him, naked and trembling with love among the scorpions and butterflies..." (page 291 of the Harper Perennial edition, translated by Gregory Rabassa).

"If whiteness is named" (p.62):

Another poem written in "espinela": ten lines structured as ABBAACCDDC in its original Spanish. Fortunately, we have been able to preserve the rhymes in translation and its lovely incantatory tone.

In *Song of a foreigner* (*Canto del extranjero*, **1976**)

The epigraph is taken from the Colombian Modernist poet José Asunción Silva's *La voz de las cosas* ("The voice of things"), which can be translated as "If I could imprison you in my verses / Grey ghosts, as you pass".

"To Violeta's shade" (p.68):

Violeta is the name Quessep gave to an Austrian friend of his, surname Lévy, who died at twenty-five or twenty-six years of age in Venice the day Quessep and she were supposed to meet in the University of Bologna, the university where Dante had studied.

"Byblos" in "Elegy" (p.74):

One of the oldest cities of Lebanon and, it has been suggested, the oldest continuously inhabited city of the world. Nowadays it also goes by the Arabic name Jubayl.

"Of blue as murmur heard" in "Elegy" (p.74):

The colour blue is a constant presence in Quessep's poetry and its varied significance is related to the Middle Eastern origin of Quessep's father. As Nicanor Vélez points out in his introduction to the Metamorphoses of the Garden, "the word azul [blue] comes from lazaward, "lapislázuli" ["lapis lazuli"], blue rock, of Persian origin; not only was the colour blue worn in mourning in the Arab world (…) but also lapis lazuli is Lebanon's national rock".

"Venut's beautiful word" in "Elegy" (p.74):

The name of Quessep's paternal grandmother, Venut Chadid.

"Song of a foreigner" (p.80):

This poem, which has been translated into Arabic as well, is written in the ancient metrical scheme known as the Sapphic stanza, in honour of Sappho of Lesbos, its inventor. It was favoured by such classical poets as Horace (frequently) and Catullus (only twice) in Latin. In Spanish it was first used by the poet Esteban Manuel de Villegas, of the Spanish Golden Age, but it was later also adopted by Miguel de Unamuno and Rubén Darío, from whom Quessep learnt it. Here he combines the Sapphic metre with assonantal rhyme.

It is very difficult to use an exact imitation of this form as the metrical systems of English (accentual-syllabic) and Spanish (syllabic) are completely different from Latin or Greek (quantitative). Anyway, it would be pointless to reproduce the metre exactly if the result were not a good poem. However, the salient feature of the Sapphic stanza is the short final line, consisting of one dactyl and one spondee/trochee, e.g. "whiteness of / island." In Greek and Latin the Sapphic stanza is composed of three hendecasyllabic verses and one five-syllable line at the end (also called the Adonic, which is why in Spanish this metric scheme is known as "sáfico adónico"). Quessep also uses eleven syllables for the first three lines of the stanza but seven for the Adonic. We have attempted to keep to the Classical model (five syllables – dactyl + trochee) for the Adonic, while jettisoning any fixed syllabic pattern for the first three lines, but at times have had to settle for an approximation.

In *Madrigals of life and death* (*Madrigales de vida y muerte*, 1978)

The epigraph is taken from the first line of the *Metaphysical poems* by the famous poet of the Spanish Golden Age, Francisco Quevedo. It is translated by Christopher Johnson for the University Chicago Press as "'Is any life home?' Nobody answers?".

"Violeta" in "Written for you, in your name" (p.100):

See note to 'To Violeta's shade'.

In *Preludes* (*Preludios,* 1980)

The epigraph, quoted in English in the original Spanish version, is taken from the legendary poem *Endymion* by the English Romantic John Keats.

In *Death of Merlin* (*Muerte de Merlín,* 1985)

The epigraph, quoted in Italian in the original in Spanish, is taken from a line in one of the poems of *Cuttlefish bones* (*Ossi di seppia*) by Eugenio Montale and translated as "Don't ask us for the phrase that can open worlds" by Jonathan Galassi for Farrar, Strauss and Giroux.

> "Song of the exiled" (p.138):

Nicanor Vélez states that the subject of this poem is Quessep's father. The reference to Byblos, mirroring the one in 'Elegy', which is dedicated to his father, favours this interpretation.

In *A garden and a desert* (*Un jardín y un desierto,* 1993)

The epigraph is taken from a line of the *Spiritual Canticle* by another famous poet of the Spanish Golden Age, Saint John of the Cross, who is a very important literary reference for Quessep. It can be translated as "amidst strange islands", as we have done in the poem included in this selection and named after this line.

> "green clemones' shade" in "To fade" (p.156):

Clemones are small trees that grow near the sea on the Colombian Atlantic Coast.

> "To fade, then, is the fortune of fortunes" in "To fade" (p.156):

This is a reference to two lines in one of Eugenio Montale's poems in *Cuttlefish Bones* (*Ossi di seppia*, 1925). The sentence in the original Italian is "*Svanire / è dunque la ventura delle venture*".

> "moon, mirror of time" in "White rock" (p.160):

Borges often speaks of a "Persian metaphor that says that the moon is the mirror of time" (for instance in his lecture on *Poetry* in the "Seven Nights") but we haven't been able to locate his direct source. The Persian poet must remain anonymous for now.

> "on the eve of the longest day" in "A Greek verse for Ophelia" (p.168):

This is the last line of the first part of Giorgos Seferis' poem, 'Summer Solstice'.

In *Imaginary letter (Carta imaginaria,* 1998)

The epigraph is taken from *A la poesía* ("To poetry"), a poem by written by Fernando Charry Lara, a very close friend and colleague of Quessep with whom he co-founded the poetry magazine *Golpe de dados*. The lines taken for the epigraph could be translated as "You alone, fleeting solar and lunar star,/ Watch man lose his battle./ But you alone, secret lover,/ Can compensate his defeat with your delirium.".

> "Engraved in the stone" (p.178):

Nicanor Vélez tells that Quessep wrote this poem thinking of his paternal grandmother, Venut Chadid, mentioned already in the 'Elegy' the poet wrote for his father.

> "Aldebaran" in "Engraved in the stone" (p.178):

A star named in Arabic as "the follower" (*al-debarán*), possibly because it rises near and soon after the Pleiades. In Europe during the Middle Ages it was also known as "the heart of the bull" because it is located at the centre of the Taurus constellation.

> "Ibn Hazm" in "Engraved in the stone" (p.178):

Author of a famous treatise on love written in Arab Andalusia in the XIth century: *The Ring of the Dove*.

> "Ars amandi" (p.184):

Another poem with a unique rhyme scheme in its original in Spanish: it is composed of a stanza of fifteen lines structured AABCBACDEEDFGFG. The title of the poem alludes to Ovid's famous treatise, *The Art of Love*. Quessep said this poem is an *ars poetica*, a declaration of the aesthetic principles that underlie his work.

Epigraph to "Imaginary letter" (p.186):

"Ulises no puede concluir. De nuevo en casa tiene que seguir inventando historias": a note taken from the Spanish edition of Canetti's aphorisms (*Apuntes 1973-1984*) translated by Genoveva Dieteric and edited by Galaxia Gutemberg/Círculo de Lectores in Barcelona, 2000. We have translated the Spanish note ("apunte") into English ourselves.

In *The starless air* (*El aire sin estrellas*, 2000)

The epigraph, quoted in Spanish in the original, is taken from 'Orpheus' in *Songs of Mihyar of Damascus* by the Syrian poet Adonis. It can be translated as "I am the tongue of a god that is to come / I am the charmer of dust".

"Adonai" (p.194):

Adonai is an ancient Hebrew name for God, the plural form of the Hebrew word "adon" ("*Lord*"), which was used to invoke God in prayer and in the Hebrew Bible, due to the prohibition against using the name of God ("Yhwh").

"Dinarzad" in "Wedding song" (p.198):

Scheherazade's sister in the *One Thousand and One Nights*, the one who originally devises the story-telling ploy through which her sister avoids the execution decreed by King Shahryar. At the end of the tale, Dinarzad (also called Dunyazad, Dunyazade, Dunyazatde or Dinazade) marries King Shahryar's brother, Shah Zaman, the Sultan of Samarkand, an ancient important city of the Persian Empire located in modern-day Uzbekistan.

In *Lunar ember* (*Brasa lunar*, 2004)

The epigraph, quoted in Portuguese in the original, is taken from a poem by Ricardo Reis (one of Fernando Pessoa's heteronyms) titled *Nada fica de nada. Nada somos* ("Nothing comes out of nothing. We are nothing") and can be translated as "We are stories telling stories, nothing".

> "wings without bird" and "a flight without wings" in "Diamond" (p.210):

These two quotations come from the poem 'Palabra' ('Word') that José Ángel Valente dedicated to the Spanish poet and philosopher María Zambrano, a very important literary reference for Quessep whom he had already quoted in the only prose poem of his work ("Myth and poetry", the first poem of the original edition of *Imaginary letter*).

In *Leaves of the Sybil* (*Las hojas de la Sibila*, 2006)

The epigraph, quoted in French in the original, is taken from one of Rimbaud's *Vers nouveaux et chansons* and was translated online by Wallace Fowlie as "O seasons, O castles, What soul is without blame?".

> "Simurgh" (p.234):

In *Metamorfosis del Jardín*, Nicanor Vélez transcribes a note Quessep sent him in regard to this creature: "may I refer [the reader] to the works *The Conference of Birds* and *Book of Kings* by the Persian poets Farid Uddin Attar and Ferdowsi. [The Simurgh] also appears in *The Thousand and One Nights*."

Farid Uddin Attar was a Sufi Iranian poet of the twelfth and thirteenth centuries from Nishapur, Iran.

Ferdowsi is one of the most important poets of Persian literature, particularly renowned for his epic poem *Shahnameh* ("Book of Kings"). He lived and wrote between the tenth and eleventh centuries.

> "blue and purple and scarlet, of needlework" in "Nocturnal" (p.238):

Taken from the Bible, Exodus 39:29.

> Epigraph to "Paradise story" (p.240):

"Every angel is terrifying": first line of Rilke's *Second Elegy* in the *Duino Elegies*, as translated by Stephen Mitchell for Vintage.

In *Abyss unveiled* (*Abismo revelado*, 2017)

The epigraph, quoted in English in the original Spanish version, is taken from the famous poem of that name by Dylan Thomas.

> "*Vergine madre, figlia del tuo figlio*" in "Prayer" (p.260):

Virgin Mother, daughter of thy Son": first line of the last canto of Dante's *Divine Comedy*, Paradise XXXIII, 1.

> "*In my beginning is my end*" in "Of cedar and cypress" (p.264):

First line of T. S. Eliot's 'East Coker' from his *Four Quartets*, quoted in Spanish in the original. Eliot, in turn, was quoting and reversing what Mary Stuart, Queen of Scots, embroidered ("*En ma Fin gît mon Commencement…*") on her Cloth of State while in prison in England by her cousin Queen Elizabeth I's command.

> "*downward to the sea*" in "Shipwreck" (p.268):

"*que van a dar a la mar*": taken from 'The *Coplas* on the Death of His Father, the Grand-Master of Santiago' by Jorge Manrique (1440-1479), one of the most important poems in Spanish literature. The line belongs to the fifth stanza of "the introit" and the full lines go: "Our lives are fated as the rivers / That gather downward to the sea / We know as Death" (translated by Thomas Walsh).

Acknowledgements

We would like to acknowledge *Brooklyn Rail InTranslation* magazine, where our versions of "Matter without the sound of love", "Being is not a fable", "A poet paradise's lost", "In the moon I have told", "I am lost by the song that keeps me awake", "In solitude written" and "Guilt" previously appeared in the August issue of 2018.

We would also like to acknowledge *Acumen* poetry magazine where our versions of "To become one with music", "The rock does not bloom", "As autumn falls" and "Insomnia" previously appeared in the September issue of 2018.

About the Author

Son of a Lebanese father and a mother from Bogotá, Giovanni Quessep was born in San Onofre, a small town in the Colombian Caribbean coast, in 1939. In a career that has spanned over 60 years, he has published fourteen books of original poetry. In addition, various editorials in Colombia have published several collections of his work and he has been included in many Colombian and Latin American anthologies of poetry.

Once he obtained his high school diploma, Quessep travelled to Bogota, where he enrolled in the Universidad Javeriana's Philosophy and Literature career and where he acquired a postgraduate degree in Hispano-American Literature from the Instituto Caro y Cuervo.

After living a couple of years in Europe, where he continued his literary formation, he became a teacher at the Universidad Javeriana, where he taught courses on the work of Dante, *The One Thousand and One Nights*, the Spanish poetry of the Golden Age and the works of Rubén Darío and Antonio Machado. He also founded and edited various important literature and poetry magazines such as *Golpe de dados*, *Eco* and *Revista Casa Silva*.

From 1982 Giovanni Quessep has established himself in Popayán, where he continued to give lectures in the Universidad del Cauca until his retirement in 1992. This institution granted him the title Doctor Honoris Causa in Philosophy and Literature in 1992. He also received Colombian's national award of poetry, the Premio Nacional de Poesía José Asunción Silva in 2004, the highest literary honour bestowed by the Colombian nation, in acknowledgment of a life dedicated to poetry. Finally, in 2015 he was awarded the Premio Mundial de Poesía René Char. Some of his work has already been partially translated into Portuguese, Arab, German, Italian, French, English and Greek.

Quessep's first book, *After paradise (Después del paraíso, 1961)*, is no longer in print, given that the author has always considered it a mere exercise of apprenticeship. Therefore, Quessep's current volume of work is comprised of thirteen published books of poetry:

Being is not a fable (El ser no es una fábula, 1968), Duration and legend (Duración y leyenda, 1972), Song of a foreigner (Canto del extranjero, 1976), Madrigals of life and death (Madrigales de vida y muerte, 1978), Preludes (Preludios, 1980), Death of Merlin (Muerte de Merlín, 1985), A garden and a desert (Un jardín y un desierto, 1993), Imaginary letter (Carta imaginaria, 1998), The starless air (El aire sin estrellas, 2000), Lunar ember (Brasa lunar, 2004), Leaves of the Sybil (Las hojas de la Sibila, 2006), The artist of silence (El artista del silencio, 2012) and *Abyss Unveiled (Abismo revelado. 2017).*

In 2006, a collection of his complete work up to that date was published in Spain by Galaxia Gutenberg under the title *Metamorphoses of the Garden (Metamorfosis del jardín)*, which the poet dedicated to his mother, Paulina Esguerra.

Out-Spoken Press Titles

The Games
Harry Josephine Giles

Songs My Enemy Taught Me
Joelle Taylor

To Sweeten Bitter
Raymond Antrobus

Dogtooth
Fran Lock

How You Might Know Me
Sabrina Mahfouz

Heterogeneous
New & Selected Poems
Anthony Anaxagorou

Titanic
Bridget Minamore

Out-Spoken 2015
An Anthology of Poetry
Out-Spoken Press

A Silence You Can Carry
Hibaq Osman

press@outspokenldn.com